AF478914
GO
GRAPHIC
OBSESSION
images
film
&
fonts
visual contents agency

l'agence photographique
de la réunion des musées nationaux

Orsay

Saint-Germain-en-Laye

Guimet

Versailles

Sèvres

Centre Georges Pompidou

Picasso

Hebert

Orangerie des Tuileries

Fernand Léger

Malmaison

Cluny

Le Louvre

Vence

Lille

...

www.pho

www.photo.rmn.fr

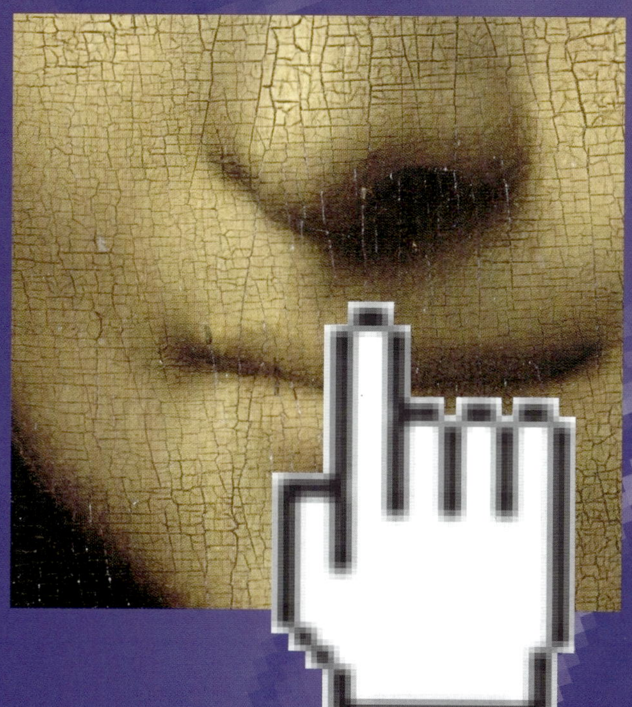

RMN
Agence photographique
10, rue de l'Abbaye
75006 Paris - France
Tel.: 33 (0)1 40 13 49 00
Fax: 33 (0)1 40 13 46 01
e-mail : photo@rmn.fr

PHOTOGRAPHY
THAT DARES

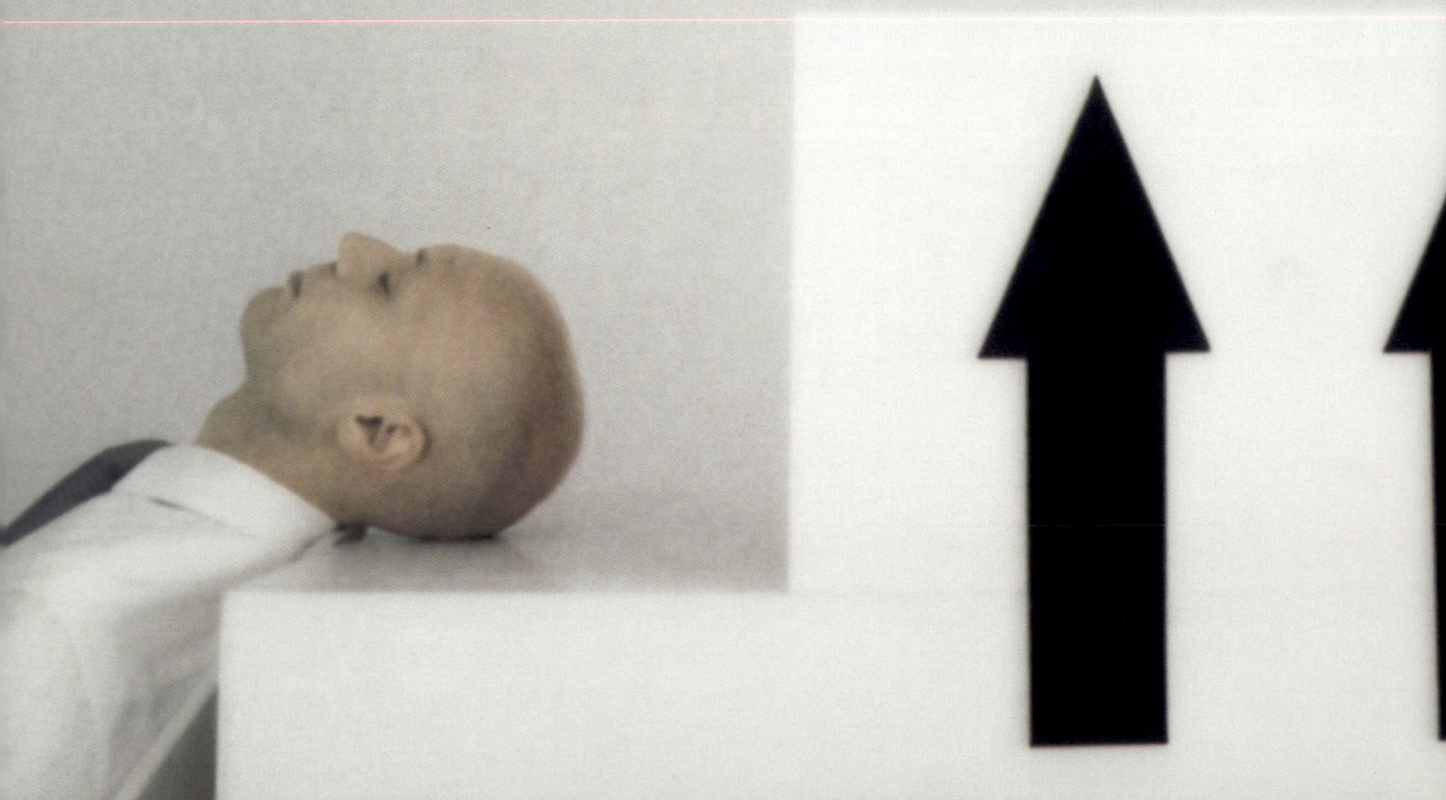

What do the five Berlin studios featured in this book
– Angela Lorenz, Atak, anschlaege.de, Cyan and
the Fons Hickmann m23 agency – have in common?
They are all on show at the 2006 Chaumont Festival,
and they each have a special and consistently
relevant relationship with graphic design.
What role does the city play in the work they create?
"Berlin isn't Germany" is a constant refrain.
Before, there were two cities, clearly demarcated
by a wall. Berlin still has a dual identity, but now
as the capital of a decentralised country and
as a cosmopolitan city with a provincial feel.
Every parcel of the city is tangibly alive with creative
activity and experimentation.
Berlin invites designers to invent their city in images
and visual adventures. This book testifies
to this incredible creative ferment.

Designed by Fons Hickmann m23

35 euros – 2-35017-035-7 – 192 pages
21 x 22.5 cm – 5 colour printing

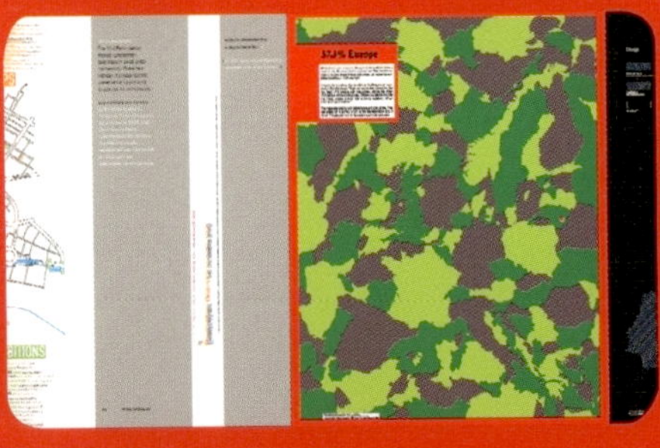
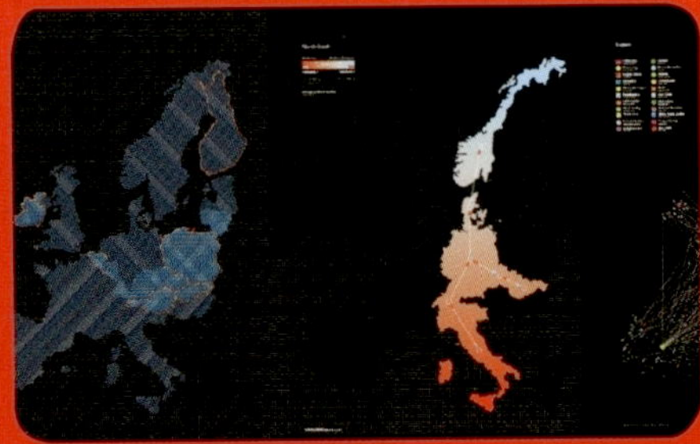

BUY THIS BOOK AT WWW.ARTDESIGN.FR

Design's the destination *by Étienne Hervy*

Companies have opened foreign outlets; set up trading posts on the trade routes, then on the communication highways; established offices abroad... Such is the corporate norm. But design is different: creatives who venture far from home can quickly lose their soul and their savings. Since the 1980s, advertising and communications agencies have grown into global groups whose economic weight is unrelated to their creative value added. That leaves the indies: agencies and freelances whose work is often partly rooted in a local context and its culture. In the 1960s, borne by universalist momentum and some cutting-edge recipes, the Swiss school exported its talents. The youthfulness of these people – their curiosity and adaptability – was definitely a precious asset. And it still is, in comparable and ever-more-numerous adventures that begin with training in foreign schools.

The tale of Dutchman Rudy Vanderlans and Czech woman Zuzana Licko reads like an American dream, and its name is apt indeed: Emigre. Some, like them, choose exile – because, perhaps, no one is a prophet in their own land. Other studios, riding their success and often evolving to fit changed personal circumstances, build bridgeheads in foreign lands. Anglo-Saxon cultural pragmatism seems to help. Studios such as Pentagram have earned strong credentials on both sides of the Atlantic. Neville Brody's Research Studios has bases in Berlin and in Paris, a city long viewed as permeable to the idea of design. Here, and elsewhere, things are opening up: young people are coming to Paris from all over Europe and Asia to cut their teeth; some are then settling here, and entering sectors forsaken by local graphic designers. Geographical origin is no longer an issue; borders mean nothing. Network organisation is no longer the preserve of the majors. The minnows are thriving on multicultural encounters, and e-conversing about work in progress. The production load can be spread without diluting the work's idea or spirit.

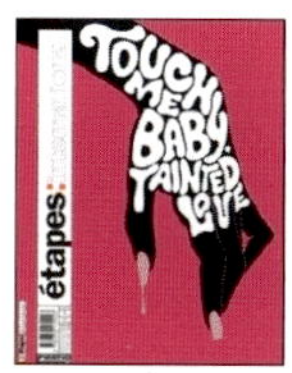

Pieter Jansen, alias Parra, works by hand to seamlessly wed imagery and text.

étapes:international

15, rue de Turbigo
75002 Paris,
France
Tel.: +33 (0)1 40 26 00 99
Fax: +33 (0)1 40 26 00 79

www.etapes.com/international

Editors & art directors
Michel Chanaud mchanaud@pyramyd.fr
Patrick Morin pmorin@pyramyd.fr

Deputy editors
Étienne Hervy ehervy@pyramyd.fr
Vanina Pinter vpinter@pyramyd.fr

Graphic and layout design
Jaga Jankowska
Karen Brunel-Lafargue, Alexis Godefroy (for the French version) Graphic and layout design © PYRAMYD

Translation
Paul Jones

Contributors
Laurent Carlier, Gérard Caron, Stéphane Darricau, Renaud Faroux, Pierre Fresnault-Deruelle, Pierre Ponant, Andréa Toucinho, Hugo van Offel, Véronique Vienne

Advertising
Advertising manager: Nadia Zanoun
nzanoun@pyramyd.fr

Subscriptions
Laurent Robic lrobic@pyramyd.fr

Publisher
Michel Chanaud mchanaud@pyramyd.fr

ISSN: 1767-47-51
© ADAGP Paris 1999 for its members' works

Printer
Saint Paul Imprimeur
38, bld Raymond Poincaré
55001 Bar le Duc, France

étapes: international is published by PYRAMYD ntcv, an SAS (company limited by shares) with capital of €110,000 whose main shareholders are Michel Chanaud and Patrick Morin.
R.C.S. Paris B 351996 509

PYRAMYD

design
FLUX

In this section, the caption body text is set in Slimbach by Robert Slimbach at ITC, www.itcfonts.com, and the bylines and URLs are in Kievit by Michael Abbink at FontFont, www.fontfont.com

Viens, ma mince, ma filiforme, ma liane émancipatrice, viens ma serpillère tordue d'amour, raz de marée d'amour diluvien, d'amour porte-drapeau rongé par l'ermine des lunaisons saignées à blanc, toute tactile du dedans, toute éponge pour le désir essoufflé du pulmoné terrestre, insatisfait de l'océan maraudeur. Toi, petit réceptacle embaumé, petite custode de chair entrouverte à l'hostie sans tache de la semence prolifique, petite chose sans nom dans le ragoût d'amour endolori de ce magma désacralisateur du ventre primitif, Épice du destin salé de l'homme profond, au coeur de lion, à la jambe de palmipède aboyeur, viens ma compresse au sourire tiède, aux dents d'horloge déchaussée dont la langue marque toujours midi-minuit, aux yeux de remontoir grinçant, trop petits pour contenir la clef du gonopode inempestif, qui fonce dans ta douceur morbide d'Immaculée Reine de la Pisse. Ô chaude fente de l'armistice entre a Chuinche et le Négrier Jaune, toi la calvaire invétérée, corrodée par l'acide prussique de la fièvre tentaculaire, roule toi dans ma joie communicative telle la poussière dans le long tapis d'Isbarnite, pour y dormir une nuit de trêve, à l'abri des chameaux ronflants, que je te barbouille du dedans d'une confiture dont une infante gavée de sucreries puisse se pâmer d'aise.

4x4 Four typefaces, four themes: love, resistance, creation and death. Each is associated with a book whose type comes alive – creating images for the poems, assaulting them, embracing them. "Les Oiseaux Tués" (Killed Birds), Adrien Aymard's end-of-course project at graphic-arts school ESAG Penninghen, is at once poetic and aesthetically powerful. VP www.adrienaymard.com

Dans leurs veines infinies
je remonte le cours de la parole
jusqu'au cri primordial
je défais l'écheveau des langues
j'attrape le bout du fil et je tire
pour libérer la musique et la
lumière l'image se rend à moi j'en
fais les bourgeons qui me plaisent

8

mort
saisit
sans
exception

Inside out At first glance, these are innocent, disadvantaged, sad old ladies. Look closer. The skin starts to crawl when you realise their cuddly garments are made of animal parts (tripe, intestines, etc.). The "Perishables" series by Pinar Yolaçan, a young Turkish photographer based in New York, prompts a shudder by associating human skin and edible meat. VP www.pinaryolacan.com

Blow-out Characters with drooping, dribbling shapes, continuing a bulimic style of linework, hungry for characters and words. Grégoire Dalle does practically all of his drawings on envelopes, back or front. The artist, who also does flyers, principally for Paris music venue Le Nouveau Casino, paints and collages too. VP http://moia.free.fr/

ENFER DES
ETOILES.....
IL PITENT AU
RYTHMES DE
MES ENVIES...
ROUGE DE
NOIR D'AUBE

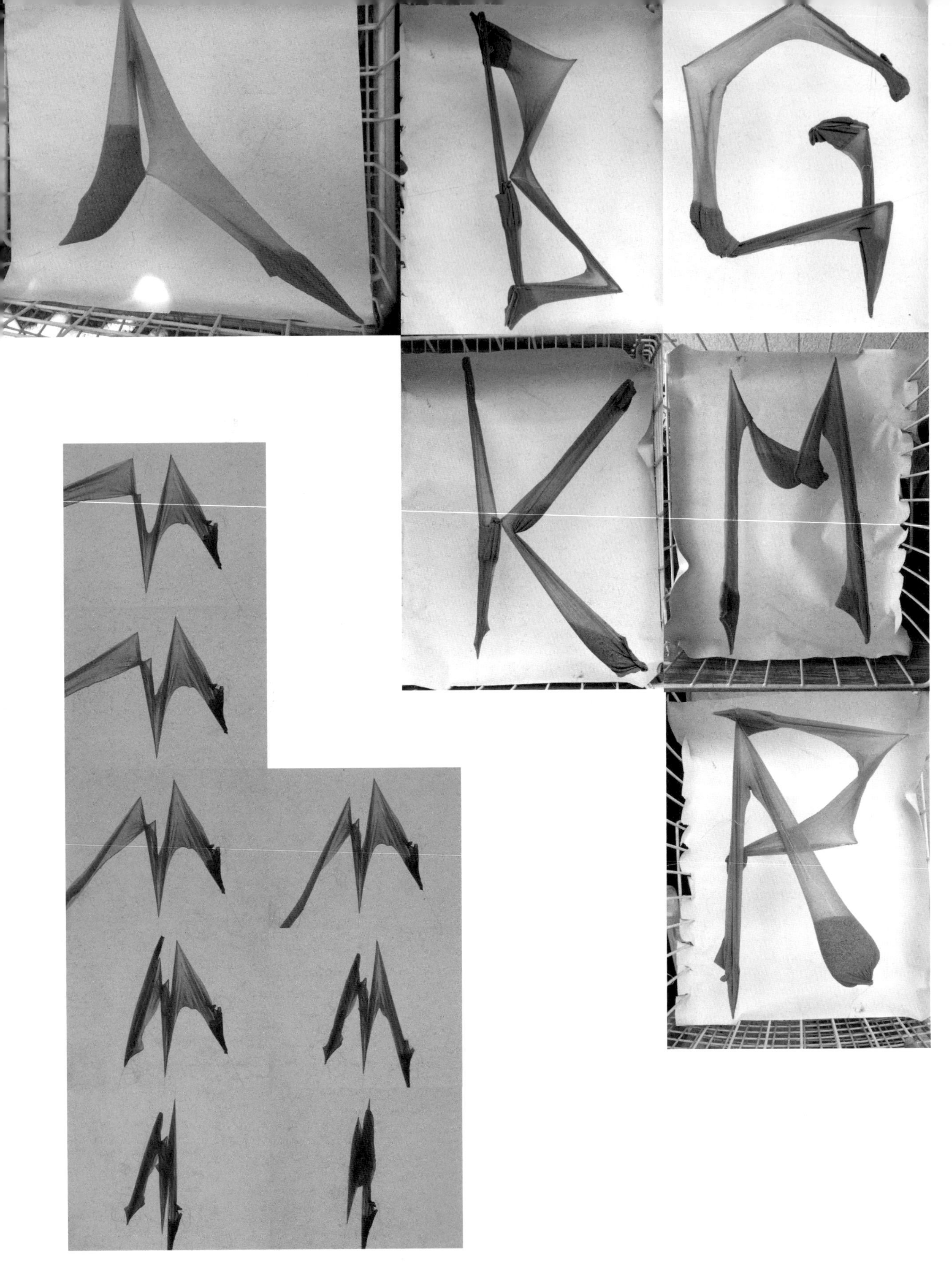

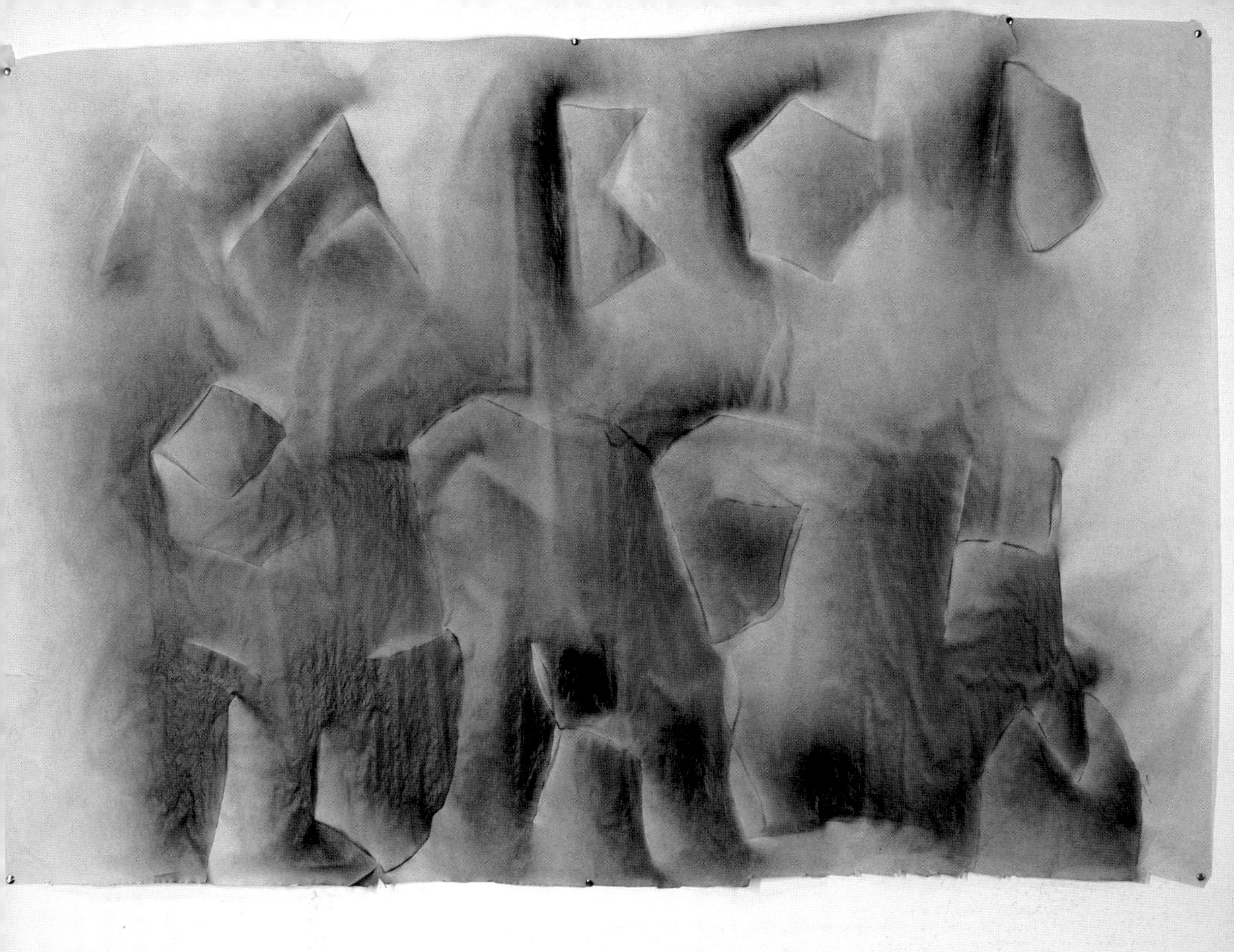

Once upon a tight These alphabets, created in workshops led by Tania Prills at the Hochschule für Gestaltung in Karlsruhe, explore the typographic virtues of textiles. Besides their material effects, the fibres' flexibility gives the curves an original tautness. Left: letters and film by Bernadette Boebel (Typo-story workshop). Right: Felix Vorreiter (Typomatinée workshop). ÉH

Home truths Since 2003, Delphine Balley has been inventing her family album. In unsettling or caustic stagings often inspired by traditional stories, her relatives, pictured in their own interiors, conceal themselves at the same time as they reveal our everyday existence in all its richness and pitifulness. Balley, represented by Lyon, France-based gallery Le Réverbère, showed her most recent series at the Paris Photo fair in November 2005. VP

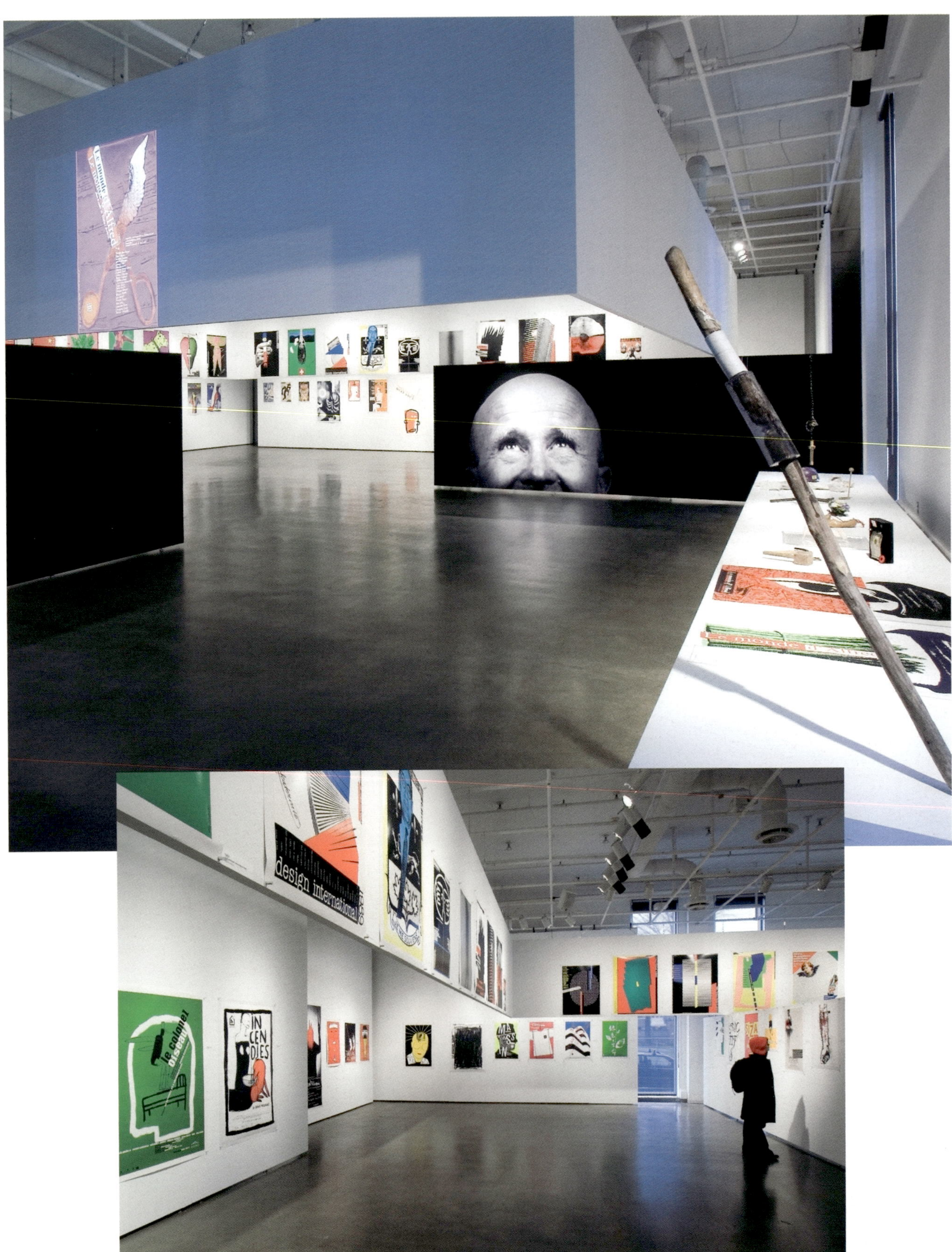

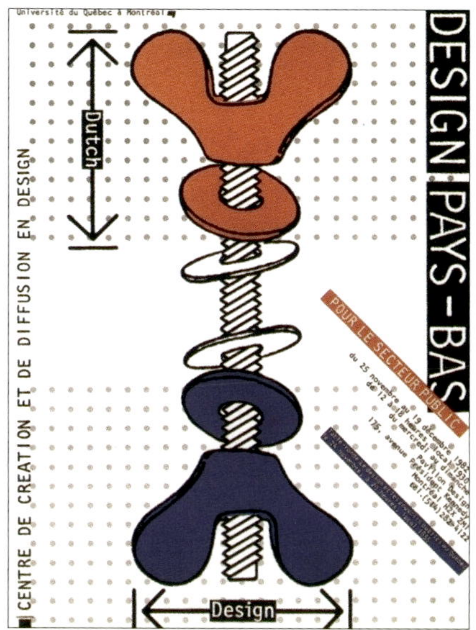

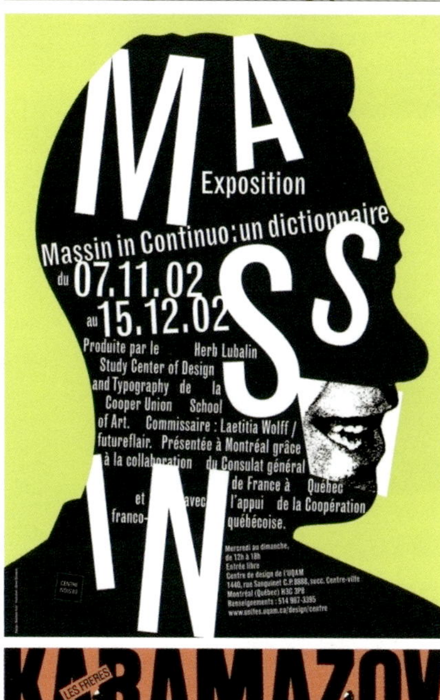

Alfred's world In late 2005, the University of Quebec at Montreal (Uqam) Design Centre paid an exhibition tribute to a professor who for over 20 years passed on a European heritage to thousands of Canadian students. Alfred Halasa, born in Poland in 1942, studied in Krakow at the academy of fine arts, architecture and industrial design. Yet at Uqam he dedicated himself to the graphic arts, with a teaching method that seemed conventional and pictorial – an organic offshoot from Tomaszewski's studio. But before focusing on this profession, Halasa had emigrated in 1973 to Paris, where he slogged away for Paris agency Esthétique Industrielle. In 1976 he moved to Canada, and a year later began working as a professor at Uqam's design school. In 1980, he founded the Bretelle graphic art laboratory with Frédéric Metz and Georges Singer; from then on he stepped up his graphic output and made a name for himself, primarily, as an *affichiste*. He had a traditional conception of posters: street art to be read immediately. His style is hard not to associate with the Polish school: drawing dominates, colours are strong (screenprinted in two or three colours), with an unfinished roughness in the linework and the treatment of signs and symbols. The exhibition tribute, curated by Marc Choko, featured 40 or so of Halasa's own posters and as many pieces by his students. The event thus reflected the power of his teaching, and his multicultural legacy to Canada. VP www.uqam.ca

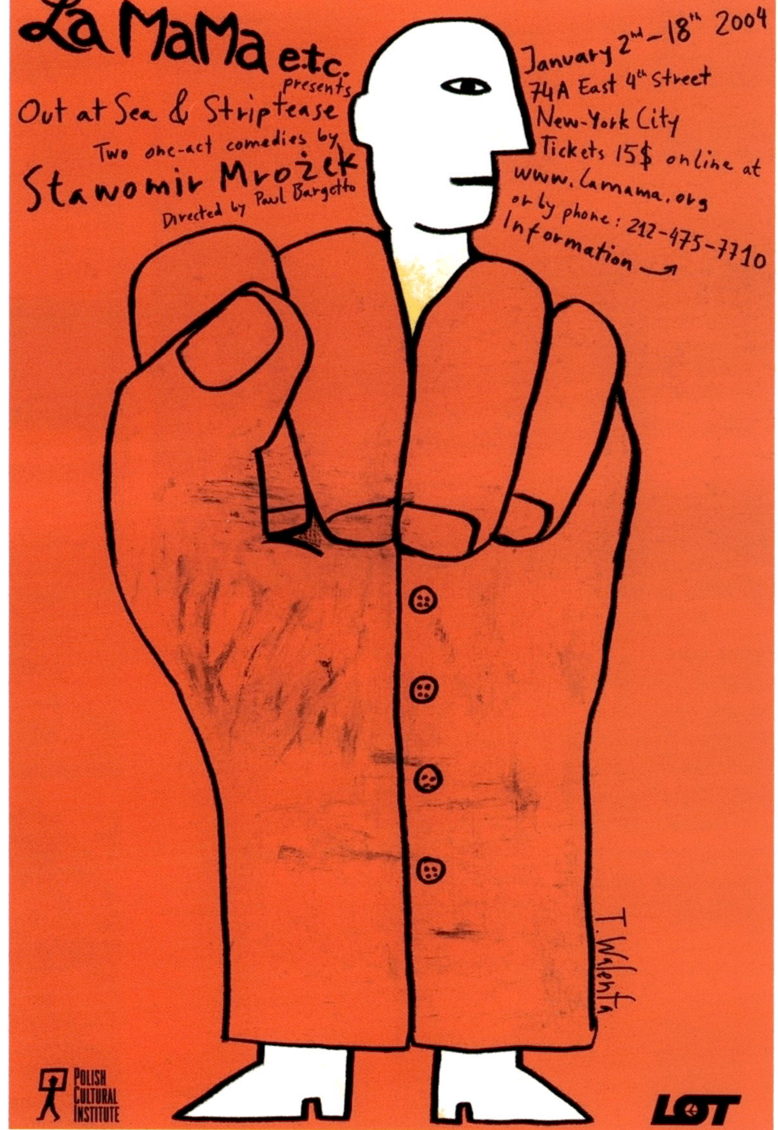

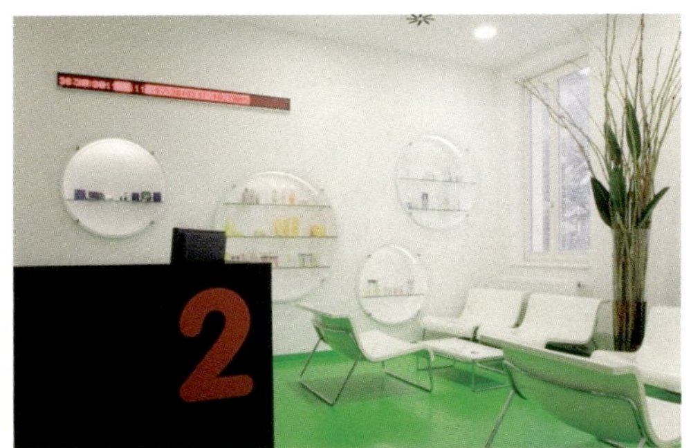

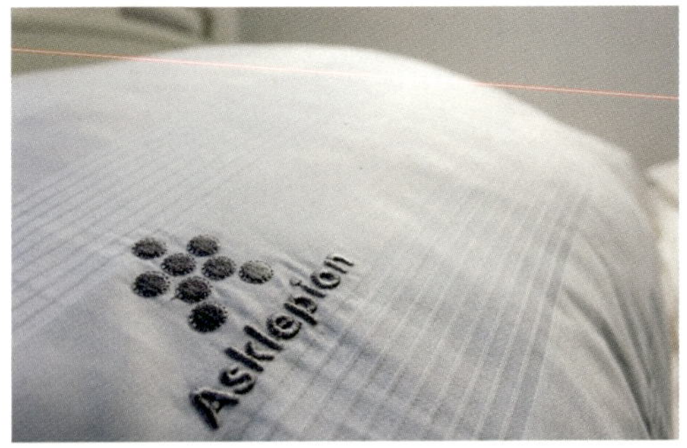

Designer care Prague-based studio Najbrt has created an identity for the Asklepion clinic that feels like a luxury hotel with a designer finish. The clinic/institute, which specialises in dental, plastic and stomach surgery and is one of the biggest in Eastern Europe, caters for patients who will need to grasp the therapeutic properties of design – if they haven't already. The logo, which is even embroidered on the pillows, represents a human body made of colour stitches, symbolising the various medical disciplines. The signage system is a long way from this antiseptic discretion, with monumental numbering that is more welcoming and almost playful. A colour system guides you between floors and specialties. VP www.najbrt.cz

The tangled web we weave

For his thesis project at the Ivrea Interaction Design Institute in Italy, Steven Blyth devised a human interface for large-screen portable phones. His virtual project, "My Social Fabric", represents the state of friends' relationships and how they are influenced by phone conversations. Each friend, acquaintance or relative is shown by an avatar inspired by the portraits of Julian Opie. The frequency of all digital communications between the user and each person, which the system monitors, determines the avatar's posture. A neglected person will gradually adopt a lethargic posture, while an alert stance indicates frequent recent contact. The avatars can be grouped manually according to sentiment, category, and so on, or programmed to begin clustering together before an upcoming event: your family before a birthday, say. Although "My Social Fabric" is a study project, Blyth has already worked for Nokia on other subjects. ÉH
www.stevenblyth.com/mysocialfabric
www.julianopie.com

A visual treaty The Treaty of Utrecht will be 300 years old in 2013. For the occasion, the city and province have already launched a wide range of events linked by a visual identity created by the Dietwee studio. Ruben Pater has designed a brown and pink language based on coats of arms; it incorporates historical and contemporary elements as well as signalling the anniversary. This creation has won a Dutch Design Award for best identity. ÉH www.dietwee.nl

CONCEPT: RUBEN PATER, TIRSO FRANCÈS, RON FAAS.
DESIGN: RUBEN PATER

Treaty of Utrecht 1713-2013

Treaty of Utrecht is a long-range international cultural event;
a joint initiative by the city and province of Utrecht that is also
supported by the Dutch government. Over the coming years,
Utrecht will feature a succession of cultural and historical
activities working towards a climax in 2013. That is the 300th
anniversary of the signing of the Treaty of Utrecht, which brought
a long period of destructive wars to an end and ushered in a
period of social and cultural progress.

Many European countries, and America too, were involved in the
conclusion of the Treaty of Utrecht in 1713. The conclusion of
that treaty was a crucial event for Europe; it showed that conflict
management could also be achieved by diplomatic means.
In 1713, the Age of the Enlightenment had already made
a cautious start and was approaching its full development.
International cooperation was increasing in both the political
and the cultural spheres.
Three centuries later, we have created a European Union for
international cooperation and conflict management. Social and
political issues such as war and peace still remain as relevant
as ever. So the Treaty of Utrecht programme will translate the
Europe of 1713 to present-day Europe.

Run, ribbon, run London-based studio GTF was inspired by a fabric memento of the Victorian era when creating this identity for the 54th Carnegie International exhibition, an event that dates back more than 100 years. Such was the motif's covering-power and adaptability that the designers rolled out temporary signage in the Carnegie Museum in Pittsburg (from October 2004 to March 2005) as well as using the ribbon – in fabric form – on the website and in the catalogue. ÉH
www.graphicthoughtfacility.com
www.cmoa.org/international

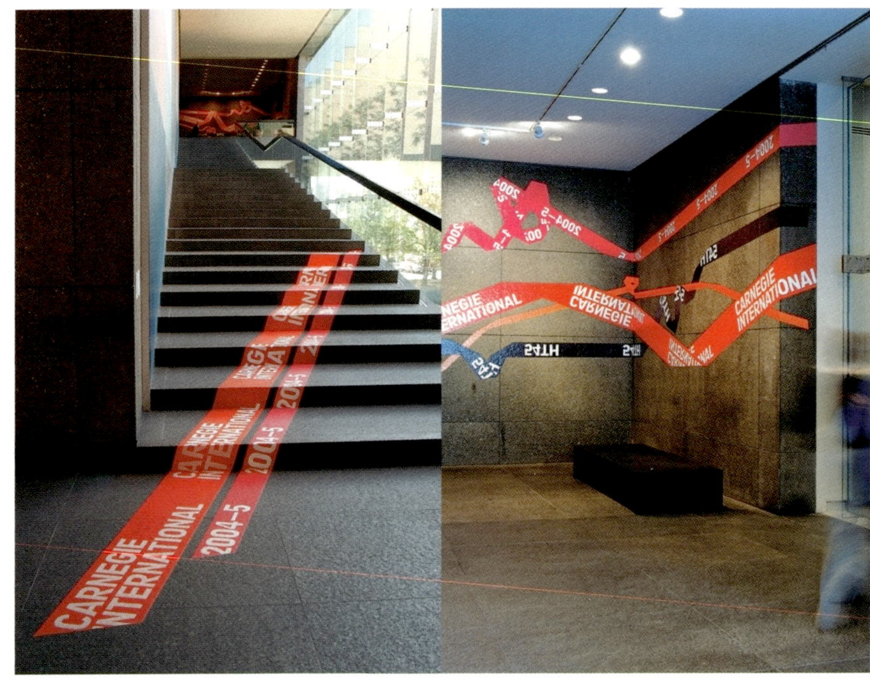

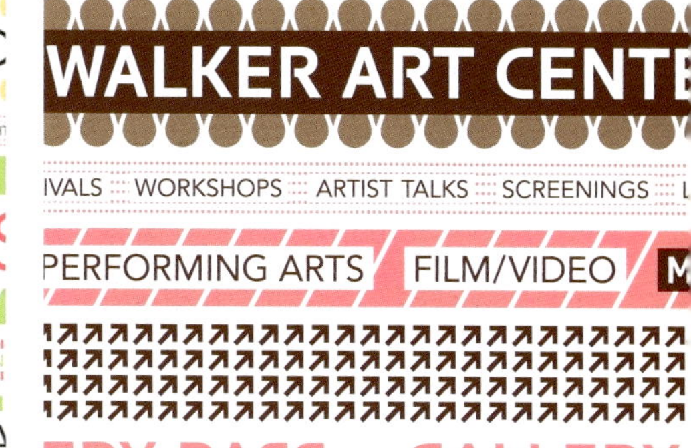

Live and unrolled Since 1995, the visual identity of the Walker Art Center in Minneapolis has been a casebook study in its use of a typeface with modular serifs as the sole signature element. After 10 years of service, the system commissioned by Laurie Haycock Makela, then director of design, is being replaced by a new script. Walker, the face designed by Matthew Carter, is still present (minus its serifs) in the system steered by Andrew Blauvelt (who succeeded Makela in 1998). Now, the basic elements are lines. Like stickytape, the identity can be deployed for tickets or branding-style approaches. The old and new identities have in common a simple language, which leverages IT and offers considerable latitude in its application – with varying degrees of ornamentation and colour. As per needs, the typeface groups keywords referring to the centre's organisation or activities. In-house team: Andrew Blauvelt, Chad Kloepfer and Emmet Byrne. Eric Olson, previously the Walker Art Center's graphic designer and the principal of Process Type, helped execute the concept. ÉH
www.walkerart.org
www.processtypefoundry.com

Packing a punch Inheriting a winemaking estate has enabled Brit Katja Thielen to innovate in the field of labelling.[1] Her plan: create a *vin à personnalité*. The visual identity is based on calligraphy, evocative of tradition. It conveys the values of craftsmanship, thus setting it apart from industrial wine production. More futuristic is the work by Japanese stylist Irie.[2] His perfume is a sort of olfactory iPod that adapts to different times of day. The design of Irie Wash revolves around the contrast between the size and style of the lettering and a black/white contrast which gives the brand standout value. Spanish studio Cosmic explores a new type of packaging.[3] Texturas, a self-initiated project, is based on the graphic transposition of culinary techniques, chemical transformation and cosmetic purity. AT

www.togetherdesign.co.uk
www.iriewash.com
www.cosmic.es

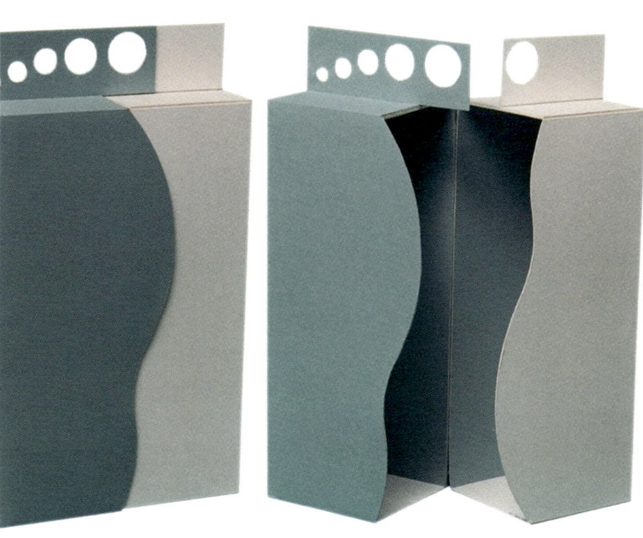

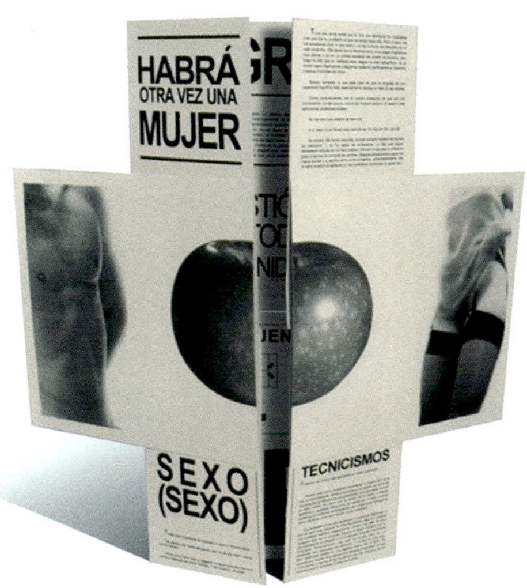

Cardboard every which way The "New packing, packaging and applications" competition is run by Procarton Espagne and the Barcelona-based industrial design association ADI FAD. It aims to promote cardboard as a creative tool. In June 2005, the event showed 100 pieces of work in three categories: student, professional and new application. The winner of this sixth edition of the event was German Blando, creator of "Larga vida al envase". Conceived to store bottles of wine, his elegant and original pack looks like a piece of sculpture. It was highly rated for its practicality, and may be commercialised. In the professional category, Drubavka Novak and Marie-Louis Van der Linden broke new ground with "Dedo ando". This shoebox received an award for its convenience and original design, which alludes to the shape of the foot. But cardboard isn't just for storage. "Querida novia" is a fun object that combines reading, play and interactive functions. Its designer Ivan Martin was specially commended in the new application category. **AT**

Fresh food for thought Here's proof to the power of three that an outfit – in this case San Francisco-based Templin Brink Design, which operates more like an agency than a studio – can reconcile creativity and the mass consumer market. Its identity for Target Store's Archer Farms food line is unusually legible and simple for the mass retail arena. The logo, which calls to mind a collection of small stickers, makes it possible to play with forms and cutouts both on printed collateral and packaging, and to create a childlike or artistic ambience. For Charles Chocolates, T.B. D. opted for discreet charm, with handmade illustrations that evoke a family brand and artisanal methods – portraying *a quality product that doesn't take itself seriously.* For the new wines by Michael Austin, the lead duo – Gaby Brink and Joel Templin – took as their starting-point the origin of the estate's name: its owners Michael and Austin. They had the idea of creating a character who has adventures that recall those of the two winemakers. *You can't compare Europe and the United States. We're not dealing with hundred-year-old companies, and many of our leading winemakers have had great success with highly creative identities.* As a result, the industry grammar can more easily be bypassed, and upping the creative ante is advised. In the same fresh vein, but with a bigger splash of humour, London agency Bloom Design portrays average consumers. A trompe-l'œil custard pie catches the attention of potential buyers, and the tub of ordinary icecream purports to conceal an... eyecatching dessert. VP

www.templinbrinkdesign.com

www.bloom-design.com

Alc 14.5% by Vol
GRAPE TAMER
Stags' Leap Ranch
Syrah
NAPA VALLEY
year..2002.
from
Michael Austin

Alc 14.1% by Vol
HIGH FLYER
Borra Vineyard
Viognier
LODI
year..2004.
from
Michael Austin

Alc 14.5% by Vol
MORAL COMPASS
Napa Valley
Syrah
NAPA VALLEY
year..2003.
from
Michael Austin

Alc 14.5% by Vol
BAD HABIT
Cabernet Sauvignon
NAPA VALLEY
year..2003.
from
Michael Austin

Charles
Chocolates
Mocha Java Pieces in
65% Bittersweet Chocolate
Net Wt. 3.4 ounces (95 grams)
Charles
Chocolates
Hazelnut and Candied Orange
Peel in 65% Bittersweet Chocolate
Net Wt. 3.4 ounces (95 grams)

WALL'S
CHOCOLATE BROWNIE
ICE CREAM DESSERT
WALL'S
BANOFFEE PIE
ICE CREAM DESSERT
WALL'S
LEMON MERINGUE
ICE CREAM DESSERT

sm's
sm's
sm's

Turning over a new leaf A tree-like, organic structure – in a green peculiar to this designer's recent work – is the basis of the design (interiors, furniture, graphic identity ranging from stationery to website) created by Matali Crasset for SM's, the museum of contemporary and decorative art in Hertogenbosch, Netherlands. In this cultural institution, the designer uproots the all-white idiom and injects cheerful hues, transposing a plant-life metaphor into the habitual white cube. Crasset's treatment gives an animate feel to the venue, housed in an old factory now converted into a cultural facility. The success of the work lies in its simplicity and homogeneous mood. VP
www.sm-s.nl www.matalicrasset.com

In this section, the titles and standfirsts are set in André Baldinger's Newut Classic (www.ambplus.com) and the body text is in Spectro by Andrea Tinnes (www.typekut.com).

___choreographics

In France, **dance** has its own official, regulated homes: the national choreographic centres. *éi* checks out these experimental venues via **five centres** and **four graphic designers** by vanina pinter

France's national choreography centres (CCN), of which there are 20, were founded in the 1980s with a specific brief: to disseminated contemporary dance locally and internationally; and to raise awareness of the discipline via programming that caters for all audiences and the creation of new work. Each centre is associated with a city and a choreographer, who is the artistic director and team leader (on a renewable three-year contract). Generally speaking, the choreographer's renown takes precedence over the location.[1] These outfits, at the experimental cutting-edge, are run by the choreographer[2] but funded by public bodies, primarily local and regional authorities. Budgets are small, and the centres are subject to considerable economic pressures and threats from their supervising ministry. They are invariably small operations with about 10 employees.

At the moment, dance is definitely one of the artistic fields that are hungriest for discipline crossovers, and close to a kind of total art. Music, costumes and stage designs are readily blended into the image-based world; projections, screens and multimedia experiences are frequently used.

In the centres, even more than in theatres, visual communication is all about encounters between two types of expertise, and how they fuse. If the two reach an understanding, the designer will respect the choreographer and be given wide creative scope. Theirs is not a formal exchange; each party is responsible for his/her discipline, but collaborating means exacting standards.

Only five choreography centres are presented here.[3] They reflect personal visions and ways of thinking about work, nurturing a graphic identity that expresses current dance trends and theories. The graphic communication here is experimental, closely linked to the personality of the choreography rather than with the venue's cultural (or programming) policy.

1) Ballet Preljocaj has substituted its name for the title Centre Chorégraphique d'Aix-en-Provence. Ditto for Mathilde Monnier, who runs the Montpellier centre.
2) As the creator, he/she has a strong personal involvement in each production.
3) Of praiseworthy note is Pierre di Sciullo's work to create the monumental signage and typography on the roof of the Centre National de la Danse de Pantin (less remarkable is the identity, by Atalante).

ÇA
GAA

The brief here was to create a set of visuals not linked to dance and the venue's programme but which, according to the brief by choreographer Daniel Larrieu, *shows that the Chorégraphiques festival now runs activities all through the year*. The imagery designed in 2001 by Manuel Warosz developed the aesthetic of a plant-like ramification which spreads throughout the poster space. And posters are just about the only medium used (on the back is information and presentation copy). Simple type (one thickness) is used, with as few sizes as possible; the information is thus graded by colour. The type is central to the poster, turning into lines that close into a labyrinth while introducing ideas of letters making gestures and being extended. This continues an idea Manuel Warosz began when art-directing an issue of *Magazine*, when he added ornamentation to Helvetica. His three CCN seasons (2001-03) respectively took the themes of plants, insects, and human physiology – a potted version of life on earth. His gaily colourful posters were a hit with the general public. *I was able to do the work because the client was responsible for it, he gave me a free hand. My images were approved first time round. You can really give massively of yourself and your time if you don't waste it redoing things.* www.antoineetmanuel.com

Four posters from three seasons. The centre's quarterly news took the form of a foldout poster with text on the back. Looking back at this work, warosz has a strange feeling. "I can no longer savour it in the same way", because many clients have subsequently requested the same style.

CCNT Choré-
graphique
3.1
respire
antoineetmanuel.com

LE CHORÉ-
GRAPHIQUE
TOURS
danse, performances, théâtre
DU 27/11 AU 05/12 2004
Informations, réservations : 02 47 36 46 00
Billetterie (MACT) : 02 47 66 17 85
CCNT
Centre chorégraphique national de Tours / Bernardo Montet

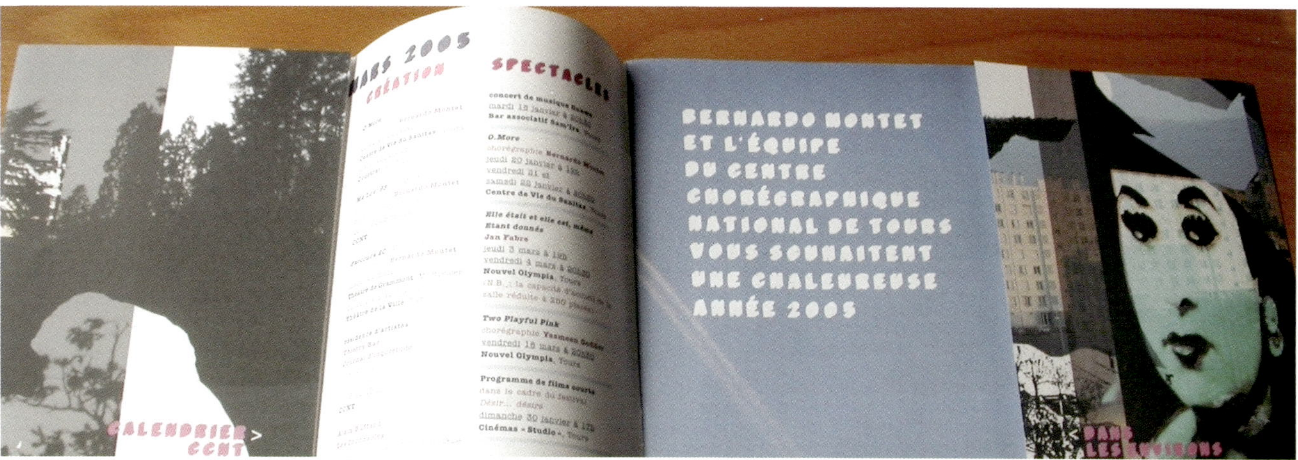

Jocelyn Cottencin's work, which echoes that of choreographer Bernardo Montet in its exploration of origins and territories, has its finger on the pulse of everyday life in Tours and its districts. Each brochure/calendar features a panoramic image that portrays the raw reality of the dance scene in Tours, punctuated with jolting dreamlike sensations. This face-off between fiction and reality scrambles expectations of the genre and its grammar. The brochures develop the idea of a notebook where the body is at play with its surroundings. Views of performances, reworked with various media, merge with the local landscape. Cottencin, like Montet, explores how a creative work can disseminate throughout an area. The CCN's identity – a piece of collage, assemblage and DIY – is something other than a fine image; it is a melting-pot of arts and genres. The attitude of Jocelyn Cottencin, and of his studio Lieux Communs (assisted by Richard Louvet), who has closer affinities with contemporary art, taps their fascination with decoding and altering our system of perceptions. www.ccntours.com

"The type for the logo was chosen to embody a sensation of heaviness, an element in architectured relief which you can enter and which destabilises the idea of a construction" (developed with Vefa Lucas). The centre's main strapline, *ça part d'ici* (it starts here), is translated into the language of the season's guest artists. The brochures hybridise images and various paper formats.

martial Damblant *Centre Chorégraphique National de Caen*

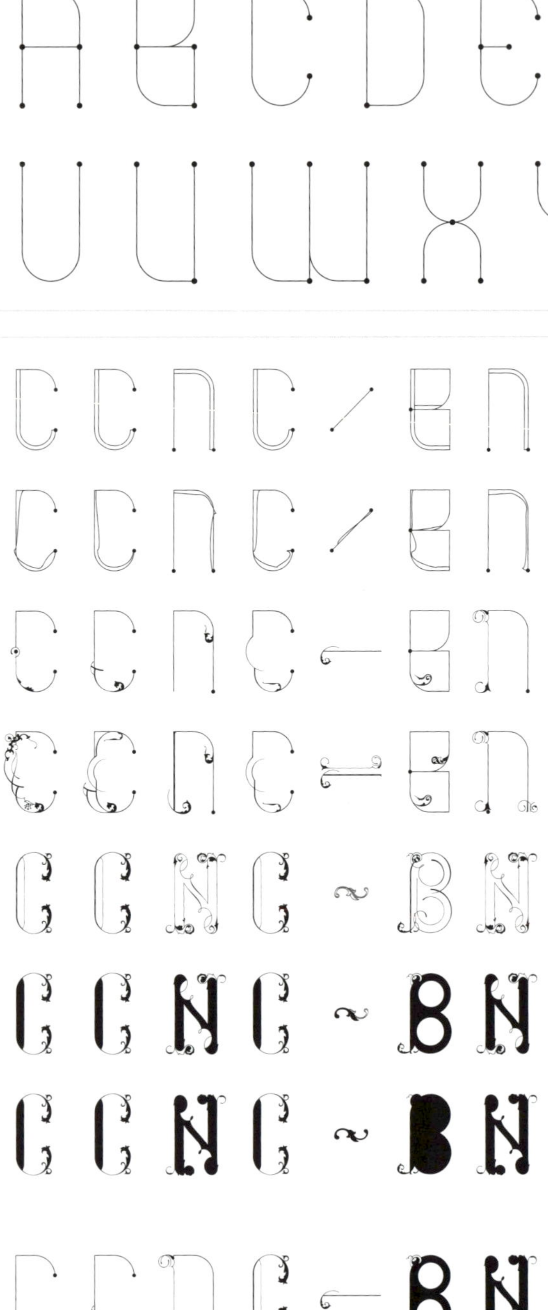

The venue's general manager put Martial Damblant in touch with artistic directors Héla Fattoumi and Éric Lamoureux: he listened to their cautious take on the body and their reticence to provoke; and thus, his approach was all gentleness and finesse. The Metz-based designer took as his starting-point the two-headed creative pairing of a Western man and a North African woman. The logo is the result of typography built on the combined basis of a circle and a square, onto which are grafted Arab-flavoured offshoots always positioned below the line (sea level) sharing the square. Taking its lead from the two artistic directors' theme, "Here and elsewhere", the logo moves symbolically from one point to another, evoking an encounter, and achieves unity between the round forms and the system of wires/lines. The discreet logo becomes a label for the centre, in a role supporting the productions, whose posters are creations in their own right. The performance topic sets the visual mood, to which other reworked typefaces are added. www.ccncbn.com

centre chorégraphique national de caen / basse-normandie

The newsletters have a vaguely marbled ground. "The mother-of-pearl of the stationery gives a softness, and contrasts with the crisp black-and-white logo." The desire to reach a wide audience has involved heavy field communication. Above right: a sheet of typographic ideas. Right: the first poster produced by Damblant, for a show titled "La Madä'a".

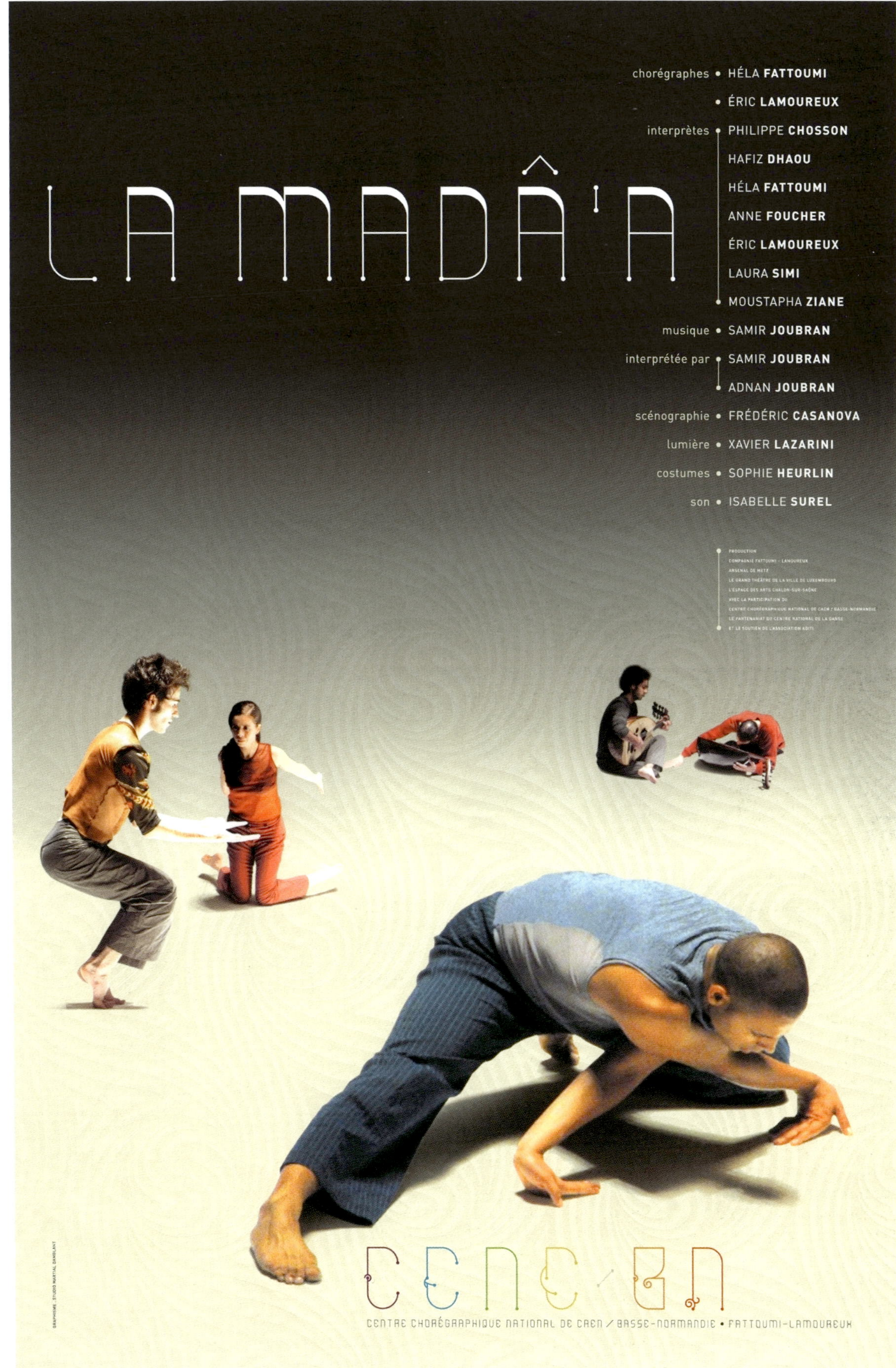

chorégraphes • HÉLA FATTOUMI
• ÉRIC LAMOUREUX
interprètes • PHILIPPE CHOSSON
HAFIZ DHAOU
HÉLA FATTOUMI
ANNE FOUCHER
ÉRIC LAMOUREUX
LAURA SIMI
• MOUSTAPHA ZIANE
musique • SAMIR JOUBRAN
interprétée par • SAMIR JOUBRAN
• ADNAN JOUBRAN
scénographie • FRÉDÉRIC CASANOVA
lumière • XAVIER LAZARINI
costumes • SOPHIE HEURLIN
son • ISABELLE SUREL
LA MADÂ'A
PRODUCTION
COMPAGNIE FATTOUMI – LAMOUREUX
ARSENAL DE METZ
LE GRAND THÉÂTRE DE LA VILLE DE LUXEMBOURG
L'ESPACE DES ARTS CHALON-SUR-SAÔNE
AVEC LA PARTICIPATION DU
CENTRE CHORÉGRAPHIQUE NATIONAL DE CAEN / BASSE-NORMANDIE
LE PARTENARIAT DU CENTRE NATIONAL DE LA DANSE
ET LE SOUTIEN DE L'ASSOCIATION ADITI
CCNC-BN
CENTRE CHORÉGRAPHIQUE NATIONAL DE CAEN / BASSE-NORMANDIE • FATTOUMI-LAMOUREUX
GRAPHISME_STUDIO MARTIAL DAMBLANT

For one poster per season, the angelic character (albeit a fallen angel) is transformed. The angel theme is an allusion to the choreographer's first name. The company's logo is by Vaughan Oliver. Facing page: flyer, 2005 New Year card and business card.

Stéphan Muntaner – when a member of the Tous des K collective – had already worked for Ballet Preljocaj, based in Aix-en-Provence since 1996; and last year he answered their call for bids. The company led by Angelin Preljocaj, which is also the core of the CCN in the Provence-Alpes-Côte d'Azur region, had decided to unify its graphics when it moved into a new building, Le Pavillon Noir, designed for the company by Rudy Ricciotti. The visual communication devised by Stéphan Muntaner is at a crossroads between two inspirations. On one hand, it directly absorbs the concrete architecture – a strong signage feature whose facade is a game of diagonals and crosses. On the other, it bespeaks the body's relationship with the choreographer's work: themes of assault, harshness and torture. The anatomy of the corps dancers is thus slashed and restitched to form a hybrid yet never bewildering ensemble. The deconstruction of the image refers to that of the body. This snipfest is also an evocation of dance in its instant ephemerality. With these dancing visuals, Stéphan Muntaner instils vibrancy and unity. www.preljocaj.org

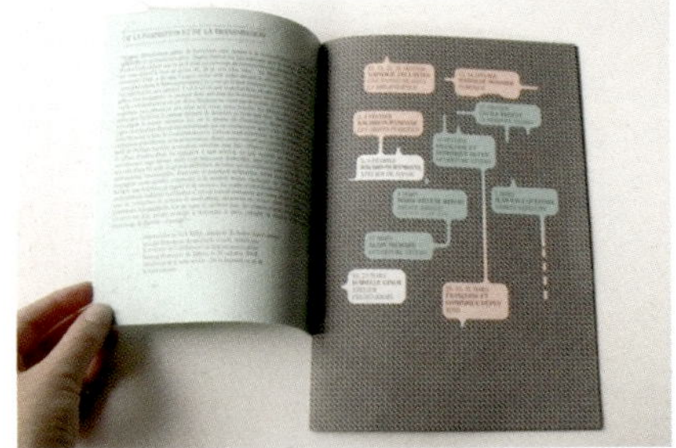

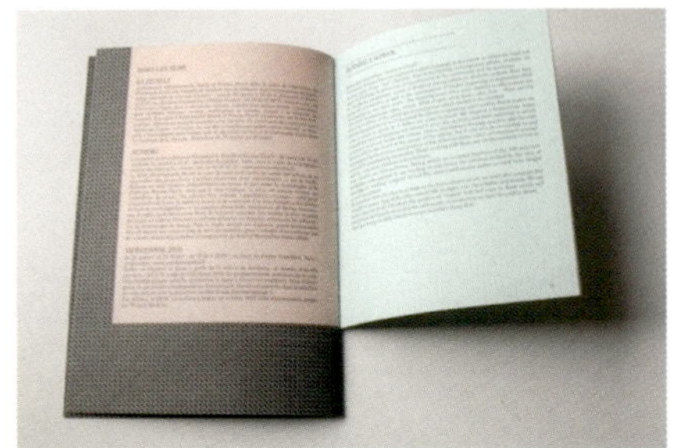

The chewing-gum logo, in variously grotesque and organic forms, calls to mind the body's fluids and internal motions. For the Centre National de Danse Contemporaine in Angers, Antoine et Manuel focused more on the pleasure an image can give than on the centre – which is specific in that it's a dance school – and the avant-garde style of choreographer Emmanuelle Huynh. After the logo, the squidgy type turns into something different in each brochure; for the most recent publication, it is made from modelling putty. The main communication collateral is a quarterly brochure, marked by a downward-leaning oblique screen whose motifs continually change. These are chosen not for their symbolism but for the way they are quirkily at variance with the seriousness of the texts, thus lacing the whole with casual humour. Each interior consists of illustrations of shows, differently treated and interpreted from year to year, with felt tip, gouache and so on… Out of principle, Antoine et Manuel stay clear of photos and their frontality. The purpose of their work, with its dedramatising drama, is also to reach amateur enthusiasts. The duo refuses to make univocal images, preferring to convey sensations. www.cndc-angers.org

This centre produces not a season poster but posters for stagings of Emmanuelle Huynh's work, in this case "Heroes". The quarterly brochure is in three parts, each larger than the last: the first contains technical information; the second, the thoughts of professionals; and the third, with its practical information, caters more to the general public.

digits are the new digital

the new digital A phenomenon of form is shifting the spotlight back onto manual artwork – both **typography** and imagery. In a backlash to computer-generated slickness, handmade art is gatecrashing the grid **by Étienne chardon**

The 2000s heralded a new era of the 'handmade', marking a clean break with the undivided reign of 'digital' that characterised the 1990s. And so the visual arts are seeing a return to more artisanal, plastic practices. The phenomenon has several explanations: growing suspicion about the now-inevitable IT tools; creatives claiming possession of a type of expertise; the celebration of tradition; and a desire to keep work raw and real.

For the 15th Poster and Graphic Arts Festival in Chaumont in 2004, Paris-based graphic designers Rik Bas Backer and José Albergaria created a typographic composition inspired by poor urban signage, with brightly-coloured sticky tape generally used for electrical work. The poster – combining the extreme simplicity of the material with the savvy complexity of the idea – felt like a manifesto advocating a return to a more authentic, less technology-led way of conceiving images. It asserted a strand of graphic expertise that extends beyond the computer, the designer's contemporary tool of choice. These two creatives were embracing the new creed of the visual arts: create personalised objects by freeing yourself from computer-imposed stereotypes. This playful, empirical approach is evident in the work of typographer Pierre di Sciullo, whose 3D faces, particularly those in stained glass, experiment with techniques on the fringe of the image-maker's typical capability, digital or otherwise.

The discipline is freeing itself from predictable processes to explore new realms where graphic objects can be enriched. But the refusal to use computers and the return to 'manufacturing' are not necessarily part of an experimental trend; rather, they sometimes stem from a spirit of continuity. The forms of Mexican graphic designer Alejandro Magallanes (*éi: 02*) are rooted in a popular pictorial tradition that has resisted the cultural invasions

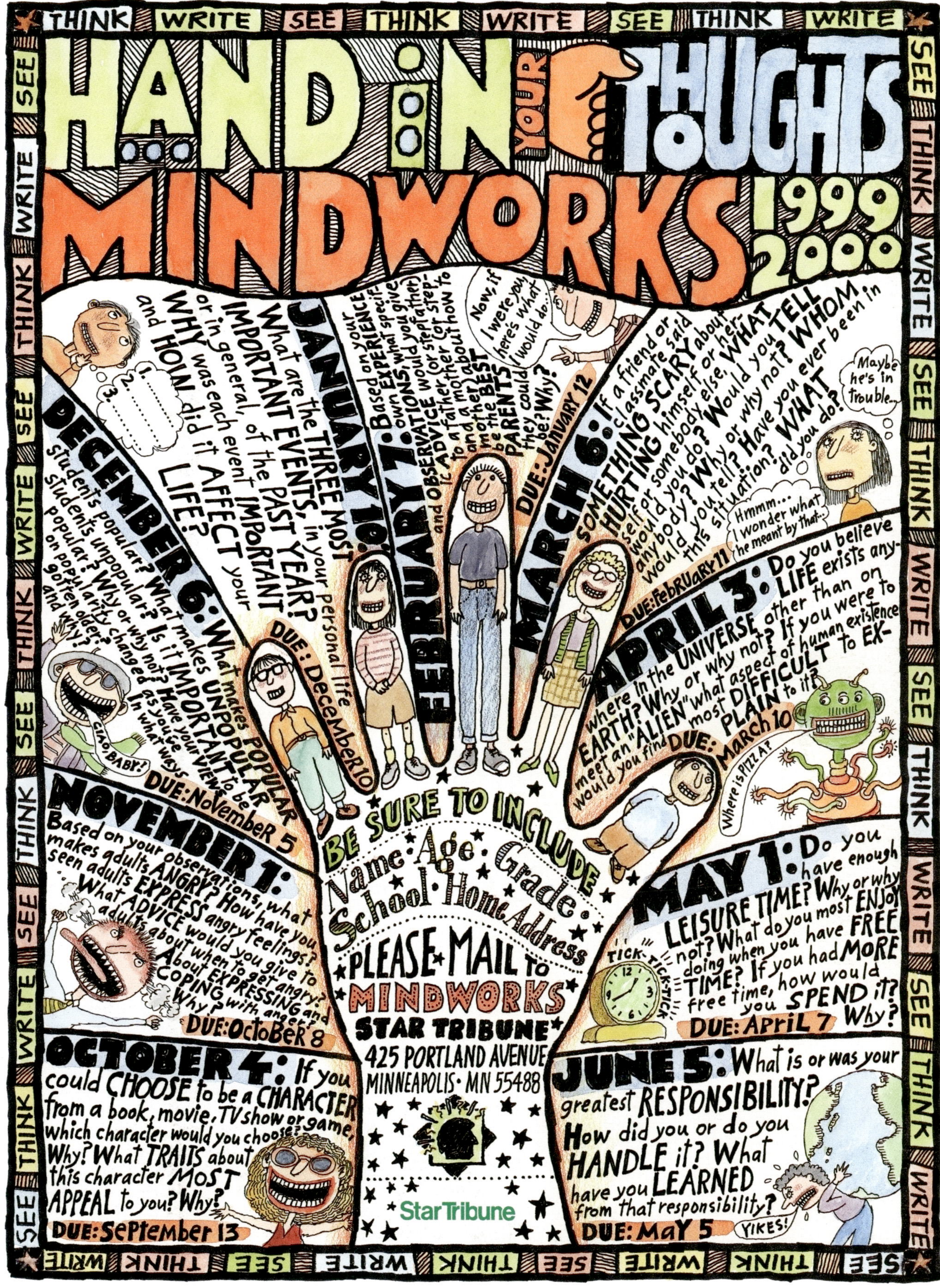
THINK WRITE SEE THINK WRITE SEE THINK WRITE
SEE THINK WRITE SEE THINK WRITE SEE THINK
HAND IN YOUR THOUGHTS
MINDWORKS 1999 2000
JANUARY 10: What are the THREE most IMPORTANT EVENTS, in your personal life or in general, of the PAST YEAR? WHY was each event IMPORTANT and HOW did it AFFECT your LIFE?
DUE: December 10
DECEMBER 6: What makes POPULAR students popular? What makes UNPOPULAR students unpopular? Why or why not? Is it IMPORTANT to be popular? Why? Have your views on popularity changed as you've gotten older? In what ways and why?
DUE: November 5
FEBRUARY 7: Based on your own EXPERIENCE and OBSERVATIONS, what specific ADVICE would you give to a mother (or step-mother), to a father (or step-father) about how to be the BEST PARENTS they could be?
DUE: January 12
Now, if I were you, here's what I would do... be? Why? Why?
MARCH 6: If a friend or classmate said something SCARY about hurting himself or herself or somebody else, WHAT would you do? Would you TELL anybody? Why or why not? WHOM would you tell? Have you ever been in this situation? WHAT did you do?
DUE: February 11
Hmmm... I wonder what he meant by that...
Maybe he's in trouble...
APRIL 3: Do you believe LIFE exists anywhere in the UNIVERSE other than on EARTH? Why or why not? If you were to meet an "ALIEN" what aspect of human existence would you find most DIFFICULT to EXPLAIN to it?
DUE: March 10
Where is PIZZA?
CIAO BABY!
NOVEMBER 1: Based on your observations, what makes adults ANGRY? How have you seen adults EXPRESS angry feelings? What ADVICE would you give to adults about when to get angry, about EXPRESSING and COPING with anger? Why?
DUE: October 8
BE SURE TO INCLUDE Name · Age · Grade · School · Home Address
PLEASE · MAIL to MINDWORKS STAR TRIBUNE
425 PORTLAND AVENUE MINNEAPOLIS · MN 55488
Star Tribune
OCTOBER 4: If you could CHOOSE to be a CHARACTER from a book, movie, TV show or game, which character would you choose? Why? What TRAITS about this character MOST APPEAL to you? Why?
DUE: September 13
MAY 1: Do you have enough LEISURE TIME? Why or why not? What do you most ENJOY doing when you have FREE TIME? If you had MORE free time, how would you SPEND it? Why?
DUE: April 7
TICK-TICK-TICK
JUNE 5: What is or was your greatest RESPONSIBILITY? How did you or do you HANDLE it? What have you LEARNED from that responsibility?
DUE: May 5
YIKES!
SEE THINK WRITE SEE THINK WRITE SEE THINK WRITE
WRITE THINK SEE WRITE THINK SEE WRITE THINK SEE

James Victore, poster for the New York School of Visual Arts, 2003.

Poster for the 20th Festival International de Danse in Montpellier, France. Graphics, lettering, illustration: Beata Jaworska. Client: Galerie Anatome.

Latin America has been enduring since the conquistadors. The technology-led aesthetic conveyed by the computer has given way to drawn, shimmering figures with a primitive flavour; in Magallanes' apparent formal naivety, some observers will doubtless sense a wish to stand firm against the cultural domination of the big American neighbour, self-absorbed behind its unscalable wall.

This desire to claim affiliation with a skill or a craft tradition is not restricted to this field, and in recent years has become increasingly tangible in contemporary art. One of the symptoms is the incredible and equally lightning-fast revival of drawing, as in the "Lee 3 Tau Ceti Central Armory Show" at Villa Arson in Nice, France, in 2002, "Draw!" at Galerie du Jour Agnès b. in Paris, and "I still believe in miracles" at the City of Paris's Museum of Modern Art in 2005. Exhibitions dedicated to the essence of artistic practice are multiplying, and even stealing the limelight from the many events about the digital arts, video and photography which as recently as the late '90s were topping the bill. Have artists grown suspicious of practices deemed too technological to be honest? No doubt. But it's also clear that today's issues are different, and that the quest for the perfect image is passé. The era of virtual reality seems to have given way to an aesthetic of fragility and subtle imperfection. Drawing, once considered a preparatory tool in the conception of a more accomplished work, is now an end in itself. More and more designers are being won over by its incomplete, 'work-in-progress' character, which is certainly more poetic and more sincere too. This imagery of ephemera takes on its full meaning in the charcoal creations of South African William Kentridge. The artist uses image-by-image animation to develop a singular dreamlike world whose cornerstone is drawing. Line becomes mark, and mark becomes movement. Incompleteness allows continuity, the next part of the story. Kentridge recreates the bond between gesture and artistic expression to such a degree that he even incorporates himself – in the process of drawing – into his films. He is thus affiliating himself with an approach both plastic and conceptual, which reinstates the humanised act of creation as an essential component of the work, on a level with the theoretical process. Freehand drawing, with its inherent hesitations, is seen as a poetic response to the slick, pasteurised images produced or retouched by computer, which have earned success for now-emblematic artists such as the German Andreas Gurski, whose monumental print-runs sent the photography market soaring late in the last century. This idea of drawing as a critical and reality-releasing tool is also an issue in today's graphic sphere. American James Victore, for example, uses photographic imagery as a creative medium and a platform for generating a new imaginative realm. In 2003, for the prestigious New York School of Visual Arts, he tweaked an anodyne portrait of a family on a beach, inserting incongruous elements such as a moustache for the father, tattoos for the children, an upturned panorama of the Big Apple, and various inscriptions – including a Rimbaud quotation and the name of the school written in a graffiti-inspired urban style, out from which a hare is leaping. This apparently chaotic profusion of signs can be read as a statement of freedom and of all the possibilities at the graphic designer's disposal. Victore's message to the school's students is simple: drawing initiates a rereading, sublimating the world of the senses and opening

william kentridge, "drawings from
journey to the moon and fragments
for georges méliès", 2003, collage, 255
x 555 cm (approx.). courtesy marian
goodman gallery, new york/paris.

cover of *everything is illuminated*.
graphics, lettering, illustration:
jonathan gray.
client: houghton mifflin books.

"Fucking A", poster for a stageplay.
graphics and lettering: Paula Scher.
client: The Public Theater.

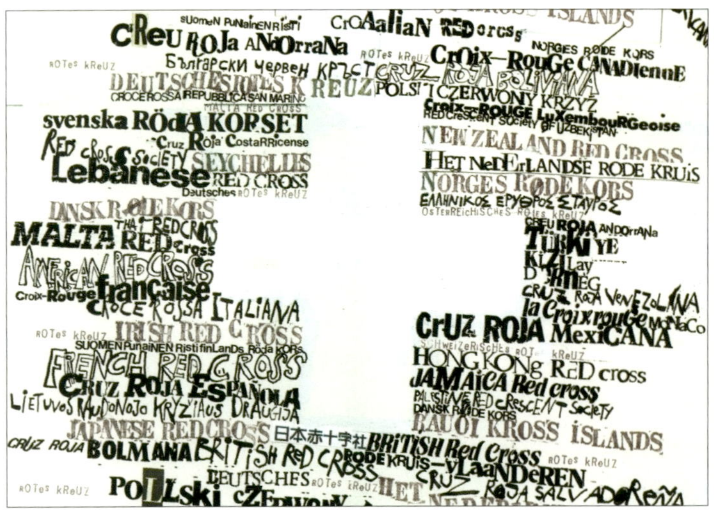

T-shirt motif for the Red Cross:
typographic references reproduced
in many languages.
graphics: spild af Tid Aps.
lettering: Jenz Koudahl.
clients: Baum und Pferdgarten,
Danish Red Cross

the doors to a new reality, a 'surreality'. Likewise typographic design, which has been almost entirely computerised since the mid-1980s invention of the Apple Macintosh, now graphic designers' preferred tool. In their recent book *Handwritten: Expressive Lettering in the Digital Age*, Steven Heller and Mirko Ilic seek to decipher the phenomenon of this alternative to conventional, software-generated type. They define cursive writing widely used by protest movements in the 20th century – American opponents of the Vietnam war, the Atelier Populaire which led the graphic front of the 1968 student uprising in France, to Iraqi resistors – as an inexpensive, popular form of expression whose authenticity supercharges the power of the message. Its apparent fragility feeds its effectiveness; and, beyond its political and militant applications, it provides an obvious formal response to digital perfection. It's clear that the growing urge to splinter off from a technology-led aesthetic goes hand in hand with an aspiration among graphic designers to distance themselves from all-conquering realism – felt to be too brutal and confining – and migrate towards a freer realm of expression where the imagination is king. But handmade images can also become a place ripe for manipulating elements within everyone's reach – as with a poster by extravagant Austro-American Stefan Sagmeister for a solo show in Japan in 2003. In the top half, the graphic designer features himself in his underpants, slouching on a sofa. In the bottom half, he's in the same position but a few kilos heavier, having consumed the foods whose packaging lies around him. Here, the poster is not an ultra-crafted, plastic composition; its virtuosity lies in its immediacy. Sagmeister removes all graphic technique and photo-manipulates everyday items in a pure pop aesthetic. As such, 'handmade' is akin to a manipulation of 'ready-made' products.

Looking beyond the savoir-faire, experimentation and overflowing imagination of their creators, handmade images and compositions are now able to escape post-production with new technology. Now they are materials to be manipulated, reused and recycled.

The Lille, France-based artists' collective Qubo Gas, to give one example, are developing a world that refers to Japanese graphic tradition. Their sketches are handdrawn or -painted, then scanned and overlaid, juxtaposed, reworked or animated. In such cases, is 'handmade' still an accurate term? It seems more like a refusal to face facts. The computer, having been the object of every fantasy and expectation, is now domesticated – and confined, like so many inventions before it, to being a tool to serve the artist and his/her palette.

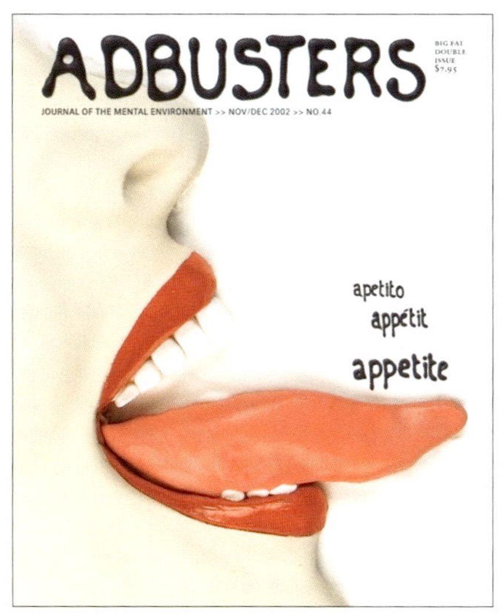

"savannah", poster by M/M for Théâtre de Lorient.

"Appetite", cover of *Adbusters*.
Graphics: Adbusters.
Cake: Dominique Jarry.
Photo: Shannon Mendes.

Qubo Gas, "Joliene", 2005. Digital pigment ink jet print on torchon paper, 55 x 70 cm. Courtesy Galerie Anne-Barrault. © Qubo Gas

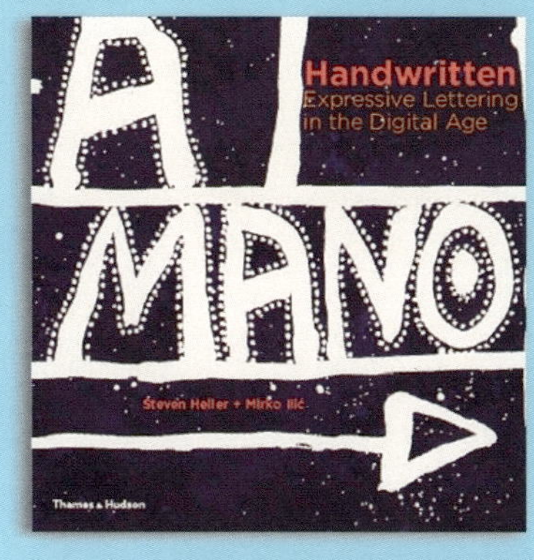

In a graphic landscape dominated by digital practices, the typographic scene has in recent years grown ripe for a return to manual letter design. From the Angus Hyland-style titles to Sagmeister scarrings, Tom Brown's boney lettering, or the child-like scripts of Tom Hautekiet, a selection of more than 500 images illustrates the analysis of this joyous and subversive contemporary phenomenon by the New York duo of journalist Steven Heller and graphic designer Mirko Ilic. They consider gestural fragility, the force of imperfection, the simple beauty of calligraphy and the insolence of experimental typography in the light of the symptoms and key trends of these new graphic vocabularies - scratched lettering, compulsive scribbles, embroidery, typeface imitations, shading and the like.

Steven Heller and Mirko Ilic
Thames & Hudson
25cm x 25cm
192 pages - Colour
Softback with flaps
£17.95

clash city painter

Though best known for his unbeatable pop art paintings, **Derek Boshier** has also been an art director, record sleeve designer, and travelling companion of rock legends like **Roxy Music**, Led Zeppelin, The Clash and David Bowie

by Renaud Faroux

Derek Boshier is an English painter who's been exiled in the United States for two decades. During the Swinging London years, he featured on magazine covers with the likes of James Dean and Elvis Presley! Since studying at the Royal College of Art, his friends had included David Hockney, Allen Jones, Peter Phillips and Patrick Caulfield, and Boshier was behind the wave of Made in England pop art that shook society in the late '60s – marked by the Mods and with a pulsating, image-dominated culture in which advertising, magazines and pop music fed an idol-hungry public.

renaud faroux — *Can you tell me about your time at the Royal College of Art in London in the 1960s?*

derek boshier — I was trying to put references to my surroundings – media and everyday objects – into my work. While studying in Somerset, I'd already taken an interest in the Kitchen Sink School represented by John Bratby, Derrick Greaves, Edward Middleditch and Jack Smith. Their work contained echoes of social realism, mixed with an existentialist view of the world influenced by the Cold War. In 1959 I painted my first flag, a variation on the Union Jack, and London started swinging!

The Air Mail Letter *series also dates from this period. In it, Derek managed a highly relevant match between painting and the printed object. The latter is copied out by hand in great detail. A scrambled Royal Mail postmark serves as proof of ID. Alert to the political issue and the loss of identity in the consumer society, he points out:* I use American images not because I like them but because of their symbolic meaning. I express the way Americanism has wormed its way into global politics and social affairs. My subjects are often inspired directly by events: the Bay of Pigs missile crisis in Cuba, the race to conquer space, the war in Iraq, the insidious dissemination of US culture and commercial interests for purposes of domination and hegemony.

I've used a lot of flag imagery for both symbolic and formal reasons. In the early 1960s, I worked on the methods of subversion that modern advertisers use to influence unwitting consumers. The industrialist David Packard defined advertisers as manipulators of symbols, and McLuhan observed that archetypal commercial images function as clusters of symbols which, when analysed, reveal multiple strata of meaning.

cover, spreads and back cover of
the clash 2nd songbook.

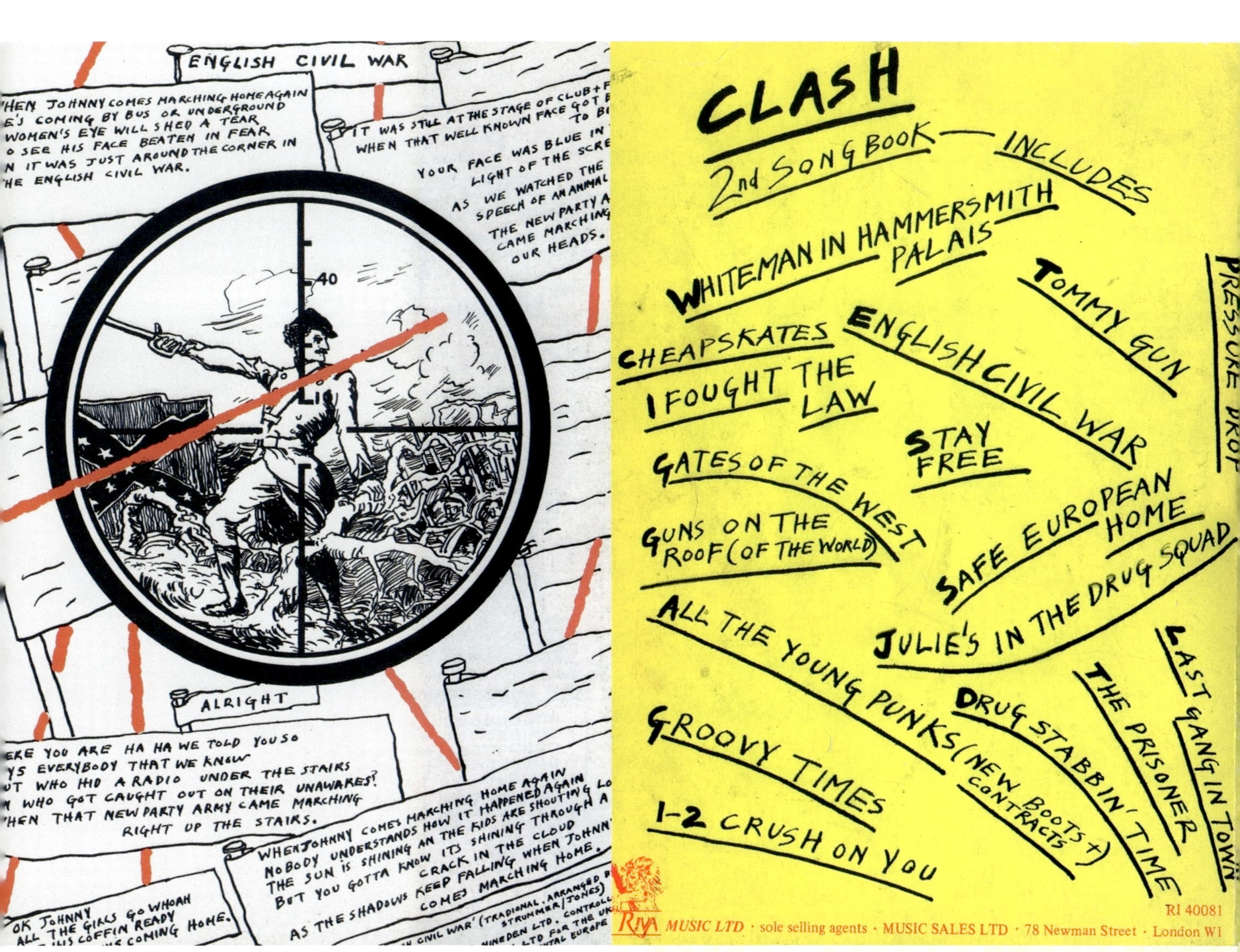

Monday January 1 1979   7p   *Short starts on page 23.*

QUEEN LIKES ....

WHAT does the Queen think about the controversial Thames Television series, Edward and Mrs. Simpson?

She is extremely distressed that the skeleton in the House of Windsor cupboard — the abdication of the uncrowned Edward VIII and all the emotional trauma it caused in the 'thirties— has been resurrected.

Continued on Page 2

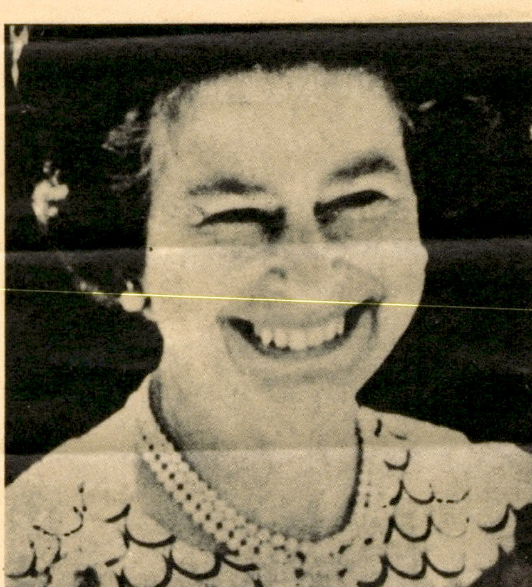

no
no
no
?
See
Page
7

WHAT'S WRONG WITH BRITAIN'S CHILDREN?

★ OUR children are turning to crime at alarming rate. They beat up old people. They cheat and lie. They set fire to schools.

★ One in five land up in the hands of the police by the time they are 18.

★ Why does it happen? Should we blame overcrowding, broken homes or television? Is it really the fault of parents?

★ The Stun has been finding out. Talking to police, psychologists, social workers, worried parents . . . and the children themselves.

★ What's wrong with Britain's children? Find out in a vital investigation, only in the Stun next week.

VIOLENCE
In Northern Ireland

£400,000 IN SOCCER'S *Battle of Britian*

No, not the I.R.A. but A VICIOUS sex fiend ripped the clothes off a 33-year-old divorcee, then beat her to death after assaulting her.

Mrs Norah Scott, ex-wife of a London barrister, was found yesterday on waste ground at Rochford, near Belfast in North Ireland.

Blood

Detective Chief Superintendent Peter Crust, head of Belfast C.I.D. said: "We are looking for a vicious killer.

"Her clothing had been ripped from her body in a most savage manner. Some of it was torn to shreds."

He added: "She had severe head injuries and there was a lot of blood." She had also been sexually assaulted.

Mrs Scott lived in a flat above her boutique called Felicity Jane in North Street—about 200 yards from where her body was found.

She had two women assistants and was well-known in the area of Belfast.

A customer said: "She was a most obliging lady the sort of person who would do anything for anyone."

Police believe the killer may be a local man who is being hidden by relatives.

Pubs

They want to interview a young man seen near the death spot — between the Old Ship and the New Ship pubs — carrying a rectangular raffia shopping basket.

Mr Crust said "He was seen in the vicinity on Monday night and we wish to exclude him from our inquiries."

Police scythed undergrowth in a search for the murder weapon.

INDIRA REVIVAL

Former Indian Premier Indira Gandhi was heading for a return to Parliament last night after polling more than half the votes counted in a South Indian by-election.

The Stun published by Derek Boshier, 25 Ladbroke Gardens, London, W.11.

FURY OVER BELFAST *HORROR* FILM FOR SCHOOLS

— Page 5

THE A-Z OF SEX

What the experts say

PLUS! PLUS! PLUS!

Jaws 2

Exclusive pictures of the film

IT'S ALL IN THE STUN NEXT WEEK

For Renaud.   Derek 2003

After work that referred to cereal boxes and the Pepsi-Cola logo, I decided to work on a new brand of toothpaste, whose selling point was the brainwave of red and white stripes. The *First Toothpaste Painting* shows a man engulfed by technology products which are completely out of control and have taken on monstrous proportions. I wanted to give a literal, amused illustration of the conditioned reflexes and 'action triggers' that advertisers use after studying the unconscious motives that drive consumers to buy things.

RF — *Can you tell me about your collaborations with The Clash?*

DB — Joe Strummer was a student of mine – apparently he hated art school! I followed his career as singer and guitarist with The Clash. One day I bumped into him in Oxford Street in London, and for a laugh I called out, "Hey Woody!" *[his nickname at art school, in tribute to Woody Guthrie]*. And he said, "I'm called Joe now!" The next day an ex-student, Caroline Koon, telephoned me: "Joe'd like you to do a book with his songs." I fancied the idea, but didn't know what he had in mind. The Clash said, "Go ahead, do it!" It was a 48-pager. They sent me the lyrics and gave me carte blanche. They only made one request, to do with the cover.

They wanted the nuclear symbol to feature somewhere. I thought about the symbol, analysed it... I'd often used logos in my pictures. I decided to use a skull tattooed with this symbol. One day I went to see Paul Simonon *[The Clash's bass player]*. He drew comics and painted too, and had a highly developed aesthetic sense. At that time, he was living in converted stables. I knocked on his door and there was silence, except for a weird whistling sound. He opened the door, and he was wearing a mask and holding a bow. On the wall there was a target – he was practising firing arrows in his lounge!

That inspired me to re-use the target in relation to the aesthetic of revolutionary violence.

The illustration I did for their song "Julie is in the drug squad" developed from a news item. At the time, the police were trying to infiltrate drug rings, and instead of hiring policewomen they were dressing bobbies up as women – hilarious, and just plain daft! I think my illustrations are directly linked to their lyrics. I tried to create images that complement the words, repeat them or respond to them. When I overlaid a banknote with the portrait of the Queen and a photo of the Duke of Edinburgh in a car that recalled the Kennedy assassination in Dallas, and stamped the whole picture with a sort of fragmented swastika, I was illustrating what people thought at the time. Punks thought all systems were fascist. Remember the Sex Pistols line, "*God save the Queen/ Her fascist regime...*" I've always liked playing on ambiguities. All my typefaces are handmade. They're the product of laziness, really, but it's become a style! I borrowed these letterings for the covers of *Lodger* and *Let's Dance* by David Bowie. If you look closely, the letters are like barbed wire. For *Lodger*, David told me to think about big bands like Glenn Miller's outfit, and think punk at the same time!

RF — *What's this cover saying? It feels like a suicide. You can also clearly see the famous photo of Che Guevara with his torturers, and Mantegna's dead Christ...*

DB — I can't really say how I ended up with this image of David. I remember how we did it technically, and the time we spent talking about it. Bowie turned up for the shoot with his hand bandaged, and he was holding a comb. Most musicians would never have done a cover with a bandaged hand and a comb. Imperfection and improvisation were our watchwords. The photographer was 'Duffy', he's now a painter. I think this is

one of Bowie's most complete albums, with tracks like "Yassassin", "DJ", "Boys Keep Swinging", "Repetition"... I'm very proud of the cover, 30 years on it works just as well! In London in 1979, punk graphics were really taking off, and I spent my time walking down the Portobello Road buying fanzines and T-shirts. Working with The Clash had a subversive influence on me. It's something I was already doing in my collages in the early '70s.

Derek Boshier still sounds English, but he left the country nearly 20 years ago for teaching posts in Houston and then Los Angeles, where he linked up again with his old Pop Art chums David Hockney and R.B. Kitaj. Derek may not have the same aura among the general public as his two illustrious peers, but his latest work is still poignantly and subversively effective.
www.derekboshier.com

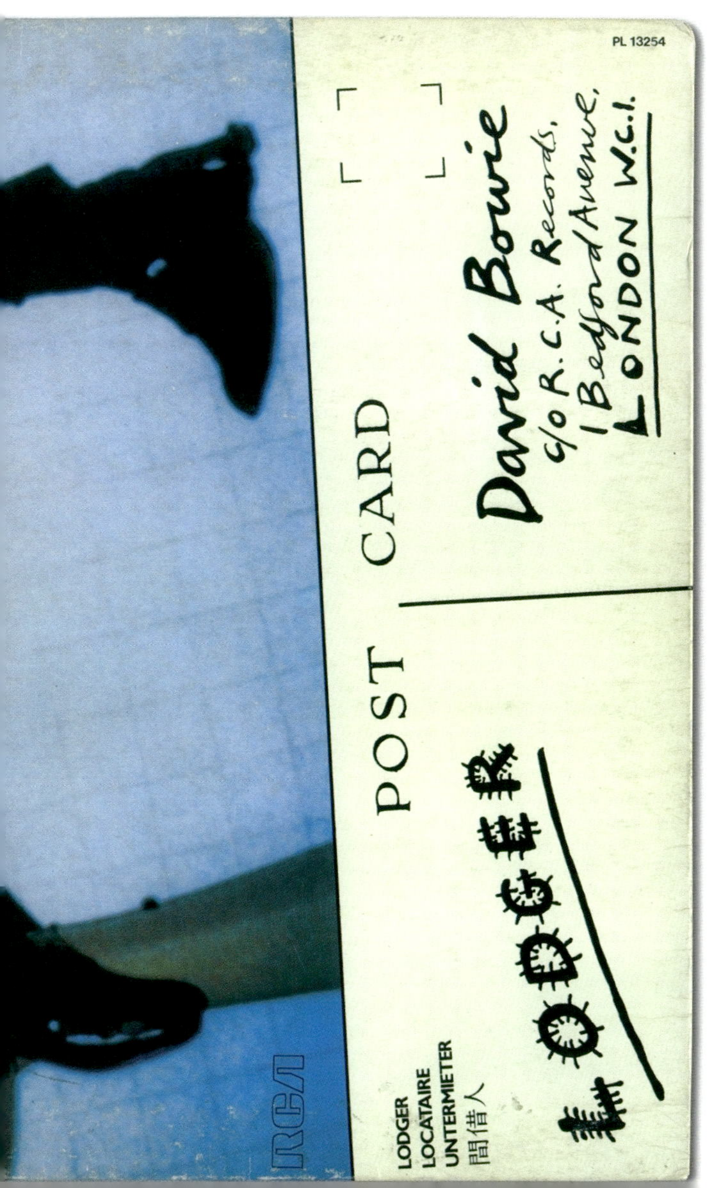

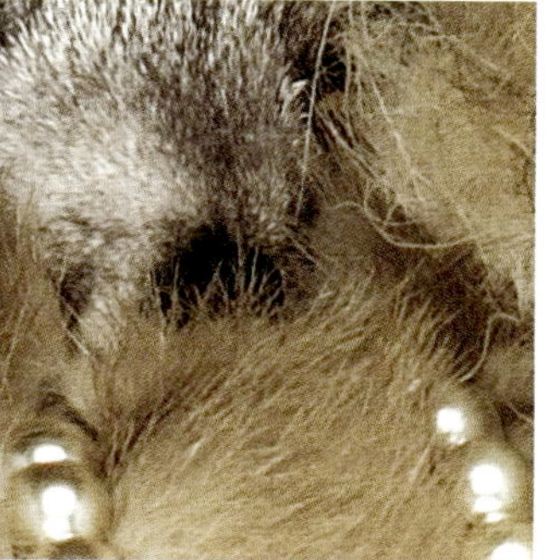

Fashioning the figure

Building on her background in styling, French visual artist Nawel is now moving into fashion imagery. She supplements the realism of photography with the expressive quality of oil painting **by vanina pinter**

Nawel. A mysterious name, androgynous or pseudonymic; a discreet step out of the spotlight with an ambiguous flavour; a non-signature attuned to the output and character of this female visual artist. Independent, voluble and determined, Nawel rejects labels and stresses how hard she finds it to define what she does. *I do illustration, but I'm not just an illustrator – like I use clothes without being a clothes designer.* Operating at the crossroads of art, fashion, and object and graphic design, Nawel blends photography, oil painting, drawing and collage. She readily describes her style as hybrid figurative. Delve

behind her naturalistic drawings and photographic memory, though, and her images render something more subtle than appearances suggest – given the other kinds of savoir-faire in the weave. To grasp their properties you need an attentive eye, and to see her work in a decent size. Her polished pictures conceal work done upstream in the creative process, during her previous activities. A fashion-design graduate of the Ecole Supérieure des Arts Appliqués, Nawel, born 1973, was taken on as an intern, then as a fashion designer, by Guy Laroche; then discovered the métier of costume designer, casting management and

production for Hermès, before becoming a press officer... During her decade in the world of fashion, Nawel continued to draw, but only in the past five years has she devoted herself to making images. Behind each commission is the expertise of a woman used to art-directing and team-working: she casts her models, works with a stylist to choose fabrics, and directs the shoots.

Nawel has been drawing since she was a kid, without ever doing it daily. She doesn't work with a clutch of scrapbooks. She is fond of oil-painting for its methodical process, which fits with a plastic-art philosophy. As with this

two images from the bahlsen poster campaign for clmbbdo (2005). the utensils and decor are photographs that can hardly be spotted in this indoor painting, thus creating material effects and unsettling perspectives.

LEFT. A series of fashion images of consummate beauty and finesse, for *sleek* (2005). In a camaïeu of white and grey, the pages feature models whose features and all of their bodies have been pencilled in. Nawel works regularly with stylist Kanako B. Koga, hairstylist Tommo Hiro and Pierrick Guenneugues of Keepcool for retouching and postproduction.

BELOW. Compositions and overlays of various photos (spread in *sleek*, 2004). Her images testify to a fascination with the body and what it expresses, as well as its physicality. Nawel likes to point out that she treats fashion as expressive material, not as a subject.

BOTTOM. Image published in *sleek*, 2005; close-up of one of her drawings.

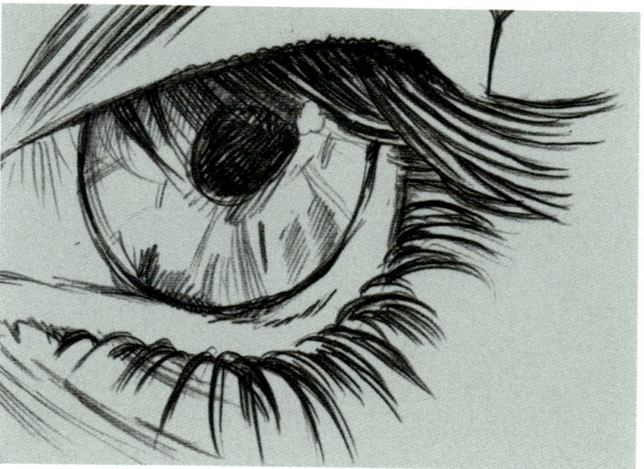

spreads from the Hermès catalogue
(30 pages, 2005). Nawel wanted to
convey a sense of profusion through
a host of stylistic treatments.
Insights into Nawel's wardrobe behind
her desk, containing her traces,
drawings, oil paints…

Above. Assemblage of photos showing the making of the Levi's campaign run in Japan.

pictorial technique, Nawel works by superposing side-by-side layers or touches; thus, t*he vibrations between the colours and strata create emotions*. And the oils merge with photos and collages... Nawel the portraitist is following in a tradition of representing personalities, sincerely and sensitively. The genre is taking her beyond the sphere of applied arts and into the fine arts, and this erects safety barriers: *I must relate the essentials without straying into complacency.*

Nawel recently did a 10-page feature for *Vogue Italia*. Her output is split between work for fashion magazines and for advertising (posters for Bahlsen and Levi's, but also the Hermès catalogues, among others). She's in no doubt she needs an agent – her current one is Dutch; many commissions fall straight into her lap, but the agent maximises her creative time. Most of her clients are from outside France (her attraction to Japan is reciprocated); recognition in France only comes after earning your spurs beyond French borders. Embodying both a return to a kind of plastic, teeming imagery (in the fashion sphere) and the porosity of genres and techniques, Nawel reflects a current trend towards figurative baroque, which, with an escalation of virtu-

osity, reaches beyond reality towards a hyperrealism heightened still further by digital technology. The figure is a dominant feature in illustration, and Nawel's stand out by their ability to capture the depths of the personality; many illustrators are content to produce the slickness of Photoshop layers. Could the return to figuration be an attempt to erase the fleetingness of techniques and trends, and of on-screen people-display methods; to restore the materiality of being? www.unit.nl

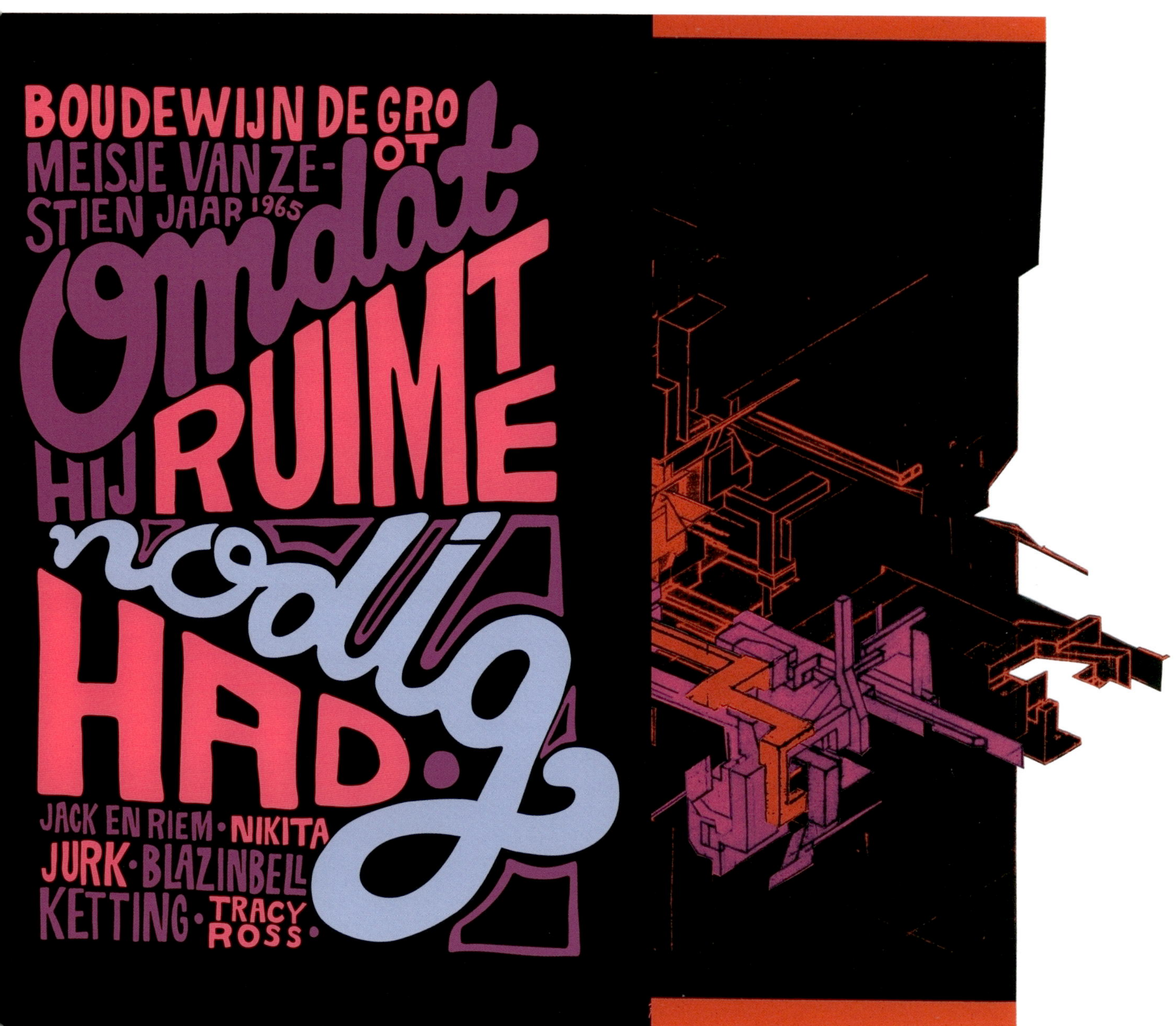

__pushing the envelope

on-screen experimentation, urban art, you name it… the visual-creative spectrum is stretching to include **new supports**, new publics and **new authorial idioms** – as illustrated here by the work of **parra**, **run**, **emovie** and **delta** by Laurent Carlier, Vanina Pinter and Hugo van Offel

eMovie →

founded: **1988**

workscope: **vjing, animated films, websites, experimental films**

location: **paris area**

websites: **www.emovie.org www.ratsi.com http://komorizone.com**

The brainchild of VJ Ratsi, eMovie is one of those shifting collectives whose members change from project to project. Olivier Ratsi (graphic design, photography, VJing), David Jungman (video), Booyo (music composition), Aurel (DJ), B^ (drawing), Sebw (photography), Nouchema (photography) and Maxime Javorsky (music composition) are blazing a trail in the underground scene and sporadically popping into the spotlight of the cultural establishment. Since 1996, they've racked up a prolific body of work (graphics, photography, video, drawing, typography, animation, music, DJing, etc.) and given material substance to fluxes mixed in VJ mode. Olivier Ratsi and David Jungman emerged from the shadows with a cross between Constructivism and experimental cinema (Booyo composes experimental music to support the images). Then the collective expanded. In 2002, *Superhighway of Lights* won the award for best interactive visual and sound show at the Flash Festival at the Pompidou Centre. For the group, interactivity is a platform for exploring randomness, for delivering a common good to an audience with an insatiable appetite for personal combinations. eMovie hurtles into the darkness of technological flaws: a bug is a precept, an accident prompts a potential: when it comes to computer calculation, cock-ups are more fertile than perfect simulation. Their output is always a group affair: they work simultaneously, in ping-pong mode, with each player contributing to a game of multimedia consequences or to an exhibition. *Visiosonor* and *Tableaux sonores* are products of this modus operandi. In his most recent series Ratsi tackles anarchitecture, with a face-off between plan elevations and random forces of gravity. He meticulously explores the time-space continuum of the senses, which he dissociates when the photos are shot. Here, representation, far from being a whim of the decisive moment, is a combination of several instants that are somehow complementary. eMovie is located in an equilibrium of fixed images and flux images that reveal the shifts of illusory immutabilities. And conversely.

1. *Pelure d'oignon* (onion peel), 2004, Ratsi. Blending flux and pause, a work on the exhaustion of forms and on random combinations of fragments, with play on depth courtesy of scale and shade perspectives.

2. *Néon sur un chameau* (Neon on a camel), 2003, Nouchema, Sebw, Ratsi and B^. Embedment of a steel-wire man with a screen head in a large number of photographs.

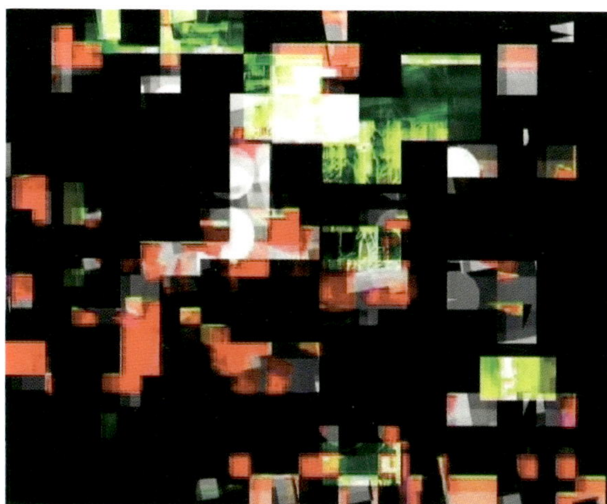

3

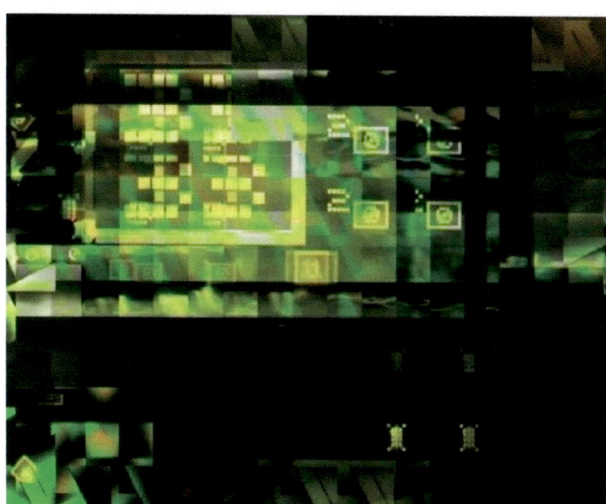

4

3. *nebula*, 2001, Booyo, Ratsi. Sound charts: (Nebula, Triptyque [Red]-G-B…): abstract animations turned into music of an experimental ambient style.
4. *vertical-horizontal*, 2001-2005, Ratsi. Deconstructed animation capture. Altered matrix synthesis: dynamic grid of entwined colour strips. The shades are determined by subtractive logic and resonance echoes between the wavelengths of the colorimetric spectrum of the composition.
5. *superhighway of lights*, 2000, Ratsi and Booyo. Movement-injected shots and iconoclastic postproduction. This experiment pushes the computer's processor to the limit.
Non-control gives rise to non-places of visual and sonic otherness.

5

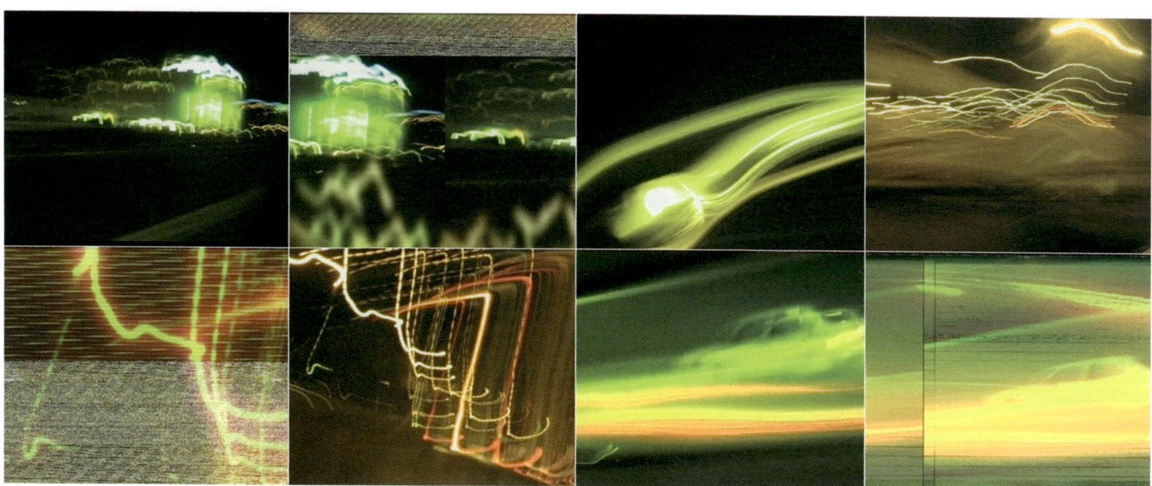

6. *Images orientées* VJ, 1998-2005,
RATSI. Mix of video fluxes, featuring
series developed autonomously. These
images are mainly articulated by cut
mixing, rather than by overprinting.

7. *Anarchitecture*, 2005, Ratsi.
The shots adapt to the tempo of the photographed actions. Small space gaps and short time gaps between shoots for fast actions; large distances with long inter-shoot gaps for slow actions.

8. Series in progress, 2005.
A chronophotographic continuation of *Anarchitecture* and *vertical-horizontal*. This approach to the everyday, via Cubism in motion and apolitical Italian Futurism, is applied to human movement.

delta →

age: **38**
workscope: **illustration, graffiti, video games, toys, painting, sculpture**
city: **Amsterdam**
website: **www.deltainc.nl**

In the land of Mondrian, the relatively uniform graffiti scene has a few maverick elements. In Amsterdam, Boris Tellegen, better known by the name of his studio, Delta, undertakes experimentation with primarily artistic and urban content with a tone of geometric abstraction that is at once consistent and powerful. He tests space and the possibilities it offers for the fragmentation and overlay of planes, and builds imaginary and improbable cities, deserted and labyrinthine (his video *YKK*, of a shifting, limitless city under construction, is a little marvel). Tellegen says he's fascinated by urban overgrowth. His cities seem to develop under control, but in fact chaos reigns... they have been forgotten. His installations and art pieces are confrontations of scales and planes – redefining the viewer's relationship with normality, disrupting the usual stability and balance. Better still, Tellegen skips from medium to medium (film, 2D, 3D) while retaining the specificity of each. Now aged 36, he starting writing graffiti at 14, then stopped for a while in 1988 to attend an industrial design school. From 1991, he managed to pluck both strings in his bow. His take on urban planning and cities is present in his supports and subjects; he staged geometric models that speak the language of urban art. A few years later, he went independent and generated his own, essentially artistic commissions, even though he enjoys the stringent demands of briefs for disc or vinyl sleeve designs.

1. Exhibition at Space Gallery, Pittsburgh. Optical play with black and white leads the eye astray between vertical and horizontal lines. The gallery's interiors and exteriors follow the same logic.

2
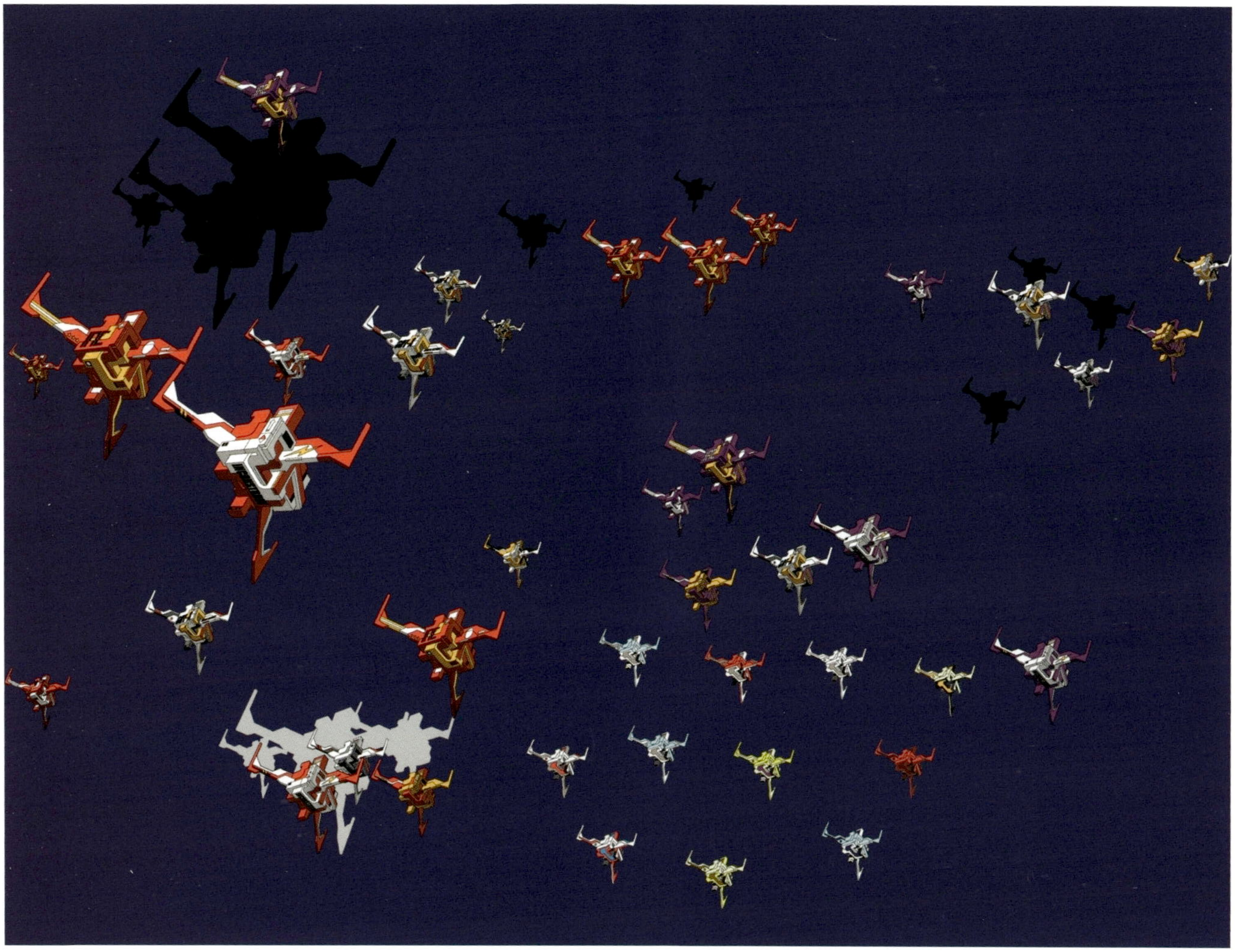

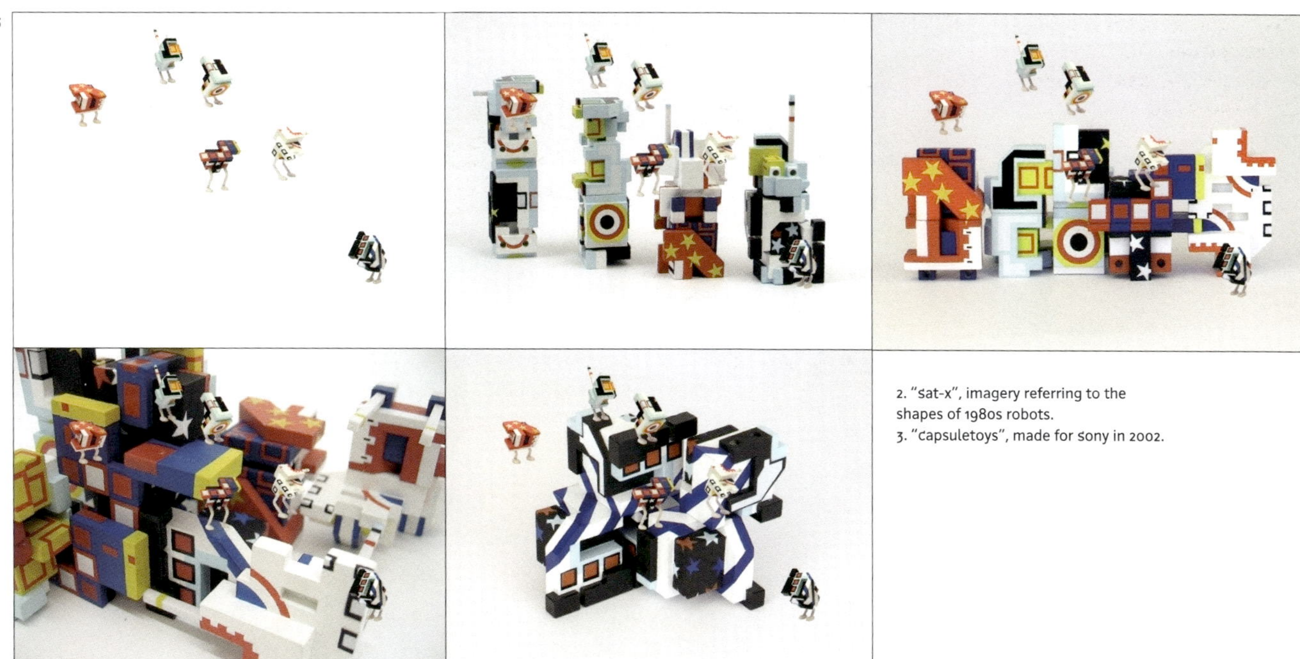

3

2. "sat-x", imagery referring to the shapes of 1980s robots.
3. "capsuletoys", made for sony in 2002.

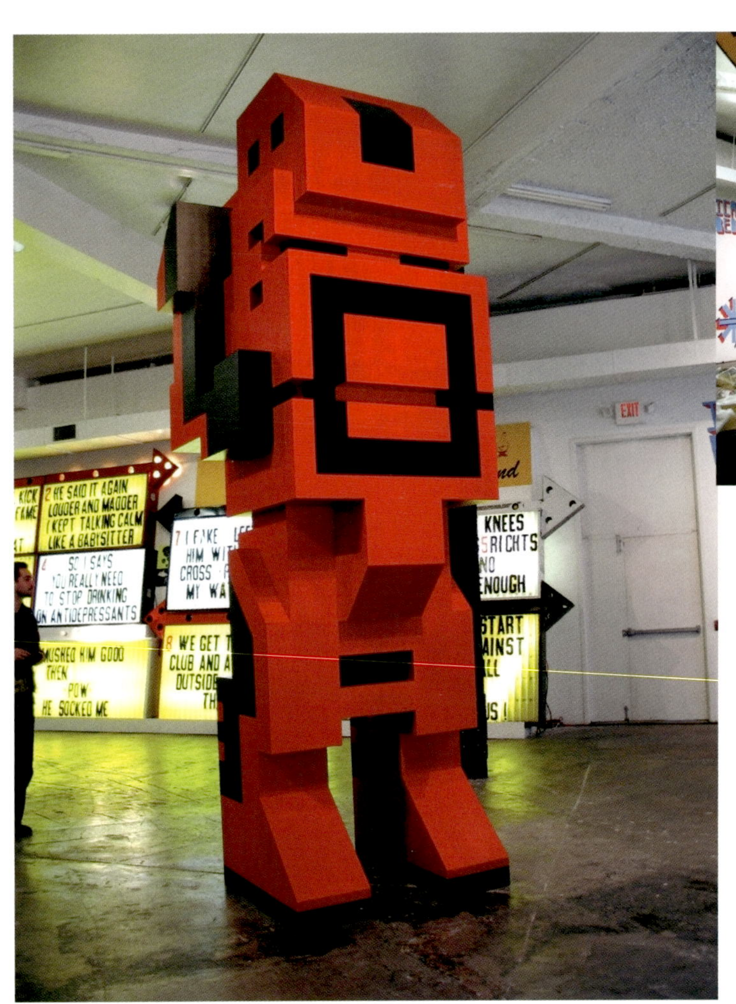

4. Recently, in the Space Gallery, Pittsburgh, Boris Tellegen erected a red wooden robot inspired by the 1980s, a nod to the period when he chose the name of his studio.
5. Disc cover for the Ann Aimee label (www.ann-aimee.net), 2004.
6. "Defumo 3", an exhibition with Mode and Futura staged in Berlin. Group black-and-white painting, with conspicuous geometric elements by Delta.
7. Disc cover for singer Aardvarck, on Dutch label Rushhour, 2004.

4

5

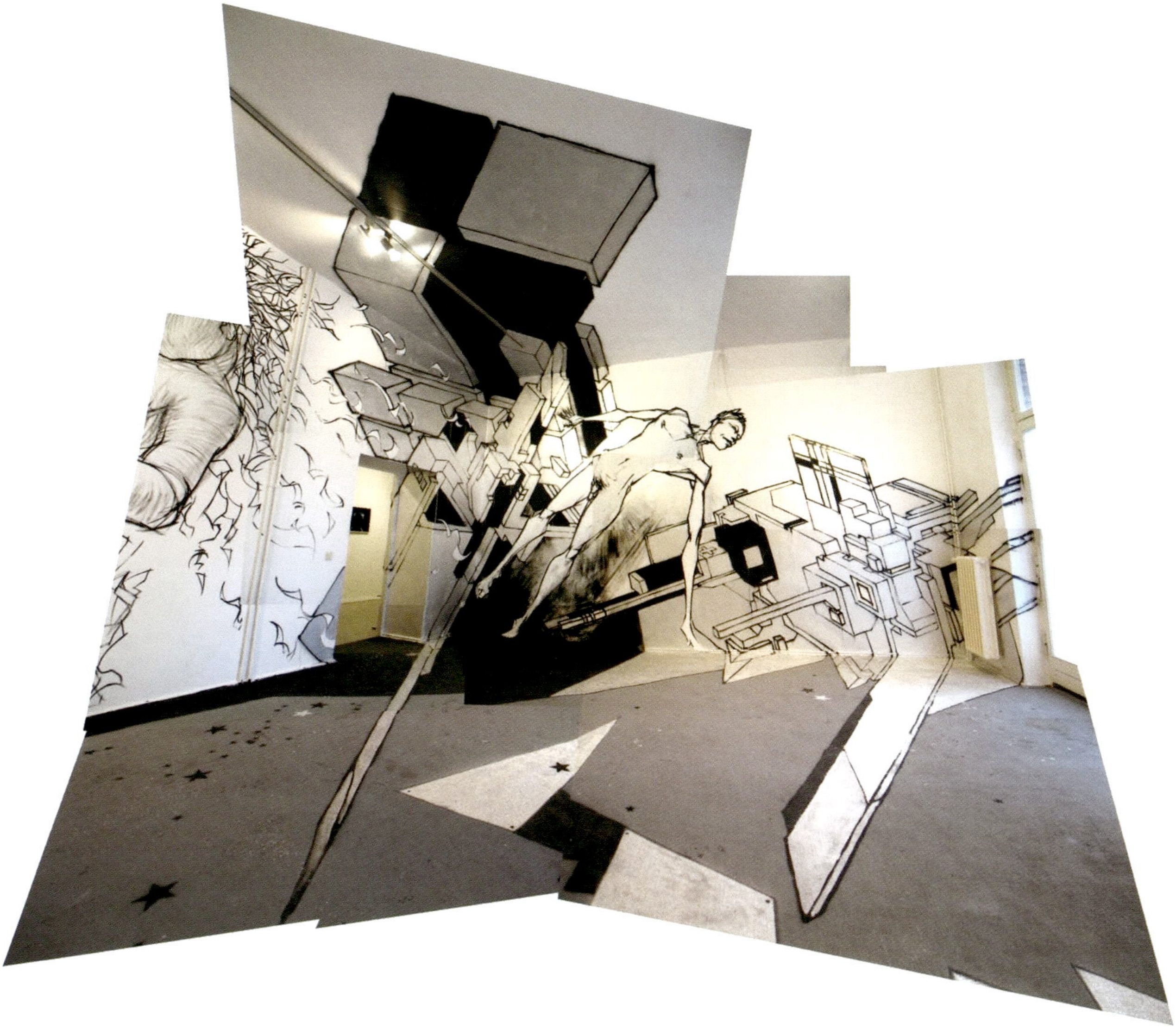

6

7

AARDVARCK CULT COPY
Side A: Cult Copy Pt 2 (original)
Side B: Cult Copy Pt 2 (Carl Craig edit)
This is part 2 of a 3 part series.
AARDVARCK
CULT COPY
PT 2 - ORIGINAL & CARL CRAIG EDIT

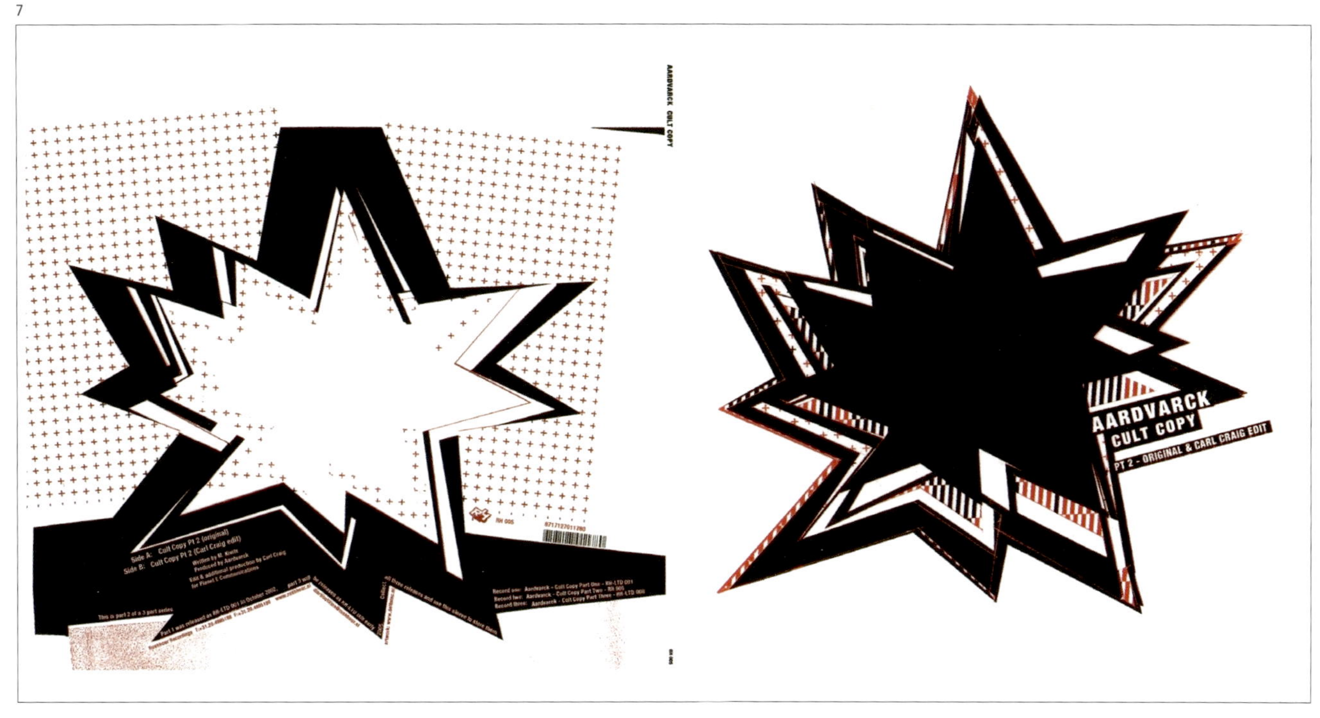

parra →

age: **29**
workscope: **illustration, posters**
city: **amsterdam**
websites: **www.bigactive.com/parra.html**
www.galeriesilo.nl/parra/

When Pieter Jansen talks about his creative journey, the narrative has a superb obviousness and freedom. Aged 22, he spent two-and-a-half years working in various advertising agencies and internet outfits. Then he suffered a bout of corporate indigestion and, with a few savings, struck out on his own with a second-hand PC. He started by creating posters and flyers for event nights in the outskirts of Amsterdam, as well as skate board designs and materials for the world of winter sports. *I began drawing more and more, using simple illustrations instead of photos [...] then I decided to design text too, and therefore I could convey a complete impression to the eye, and I had more freedom...* This self-contained output made him independent... and led to numerous commissions. Now aged 29, Pieter Jansen, alias Parra, can point to a client base including Ben & Jerry, Footlocker, Nike Europe, the London Film Festival, Volkswagen, clothing brand Rockwell, etc., and to his show at the Kemistry Gallery in London; he is now represented by UK agency Big Active. *I get my inspiration from my surroundings, the entire world is covered with text and type. What's more, I'll always be a skateboarder, and this bond with the street and pathmaking gives me a different way of looking at things.* Look at his portfolio and the Parra hallmark seems coherent and strong, but he points out: *my style is my style, but it changes monthly [...] it's developing all the time. In the place where illustration, graphic design and typography overlap [...] there are lots of possibilities and development combinations.* It's up to him to invent and regenerate his imagery.

since June 2005, parra has been working on a series of images (some feature in disc covers and flyers) for a solo show "Tits and Typo". They portray bird-faced men and scantily-clad women.
"The bird-faced character isn't the same every time. It's inspired by a strange situation between people. With bird features, the character becomes more ridiculous and strange. But I keep it like a human being, because it's more interesting if you see a certain face or hair [...] you immediately form an opinion about the person, you can immediately store it away somewhere in your mind [...] with a bird's head, it's harder to understand, and you'll look at the situation and text first, without being distracted by a human face. [...] sometimes I do dog or rabbit heads, it depends what kind of mood I'm in."

FUC
ALL

GET
ME A
GLASS
YOU
TWAT.
CU
NT

the VERY
BEST OF
Pals.

GET
ME A
GLASS
YOU
TWAT.
CU
NT

LILIAN
CANNOT USE
THE PHONE

R
D

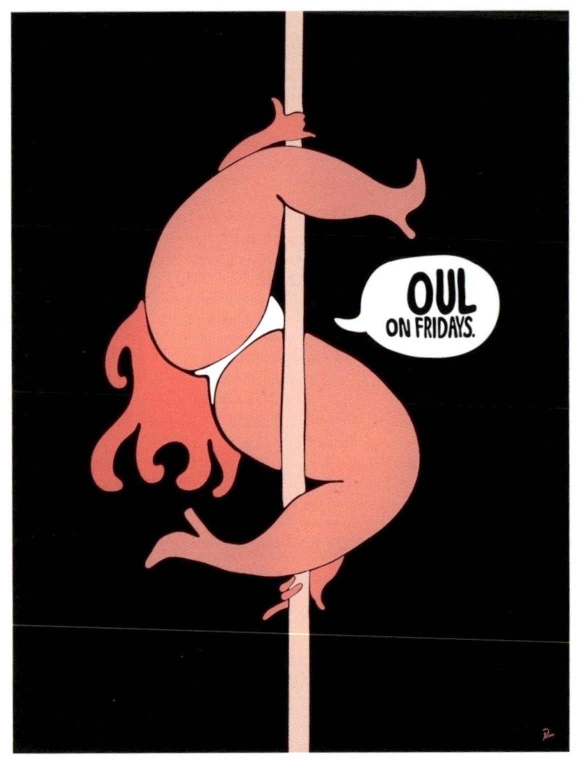

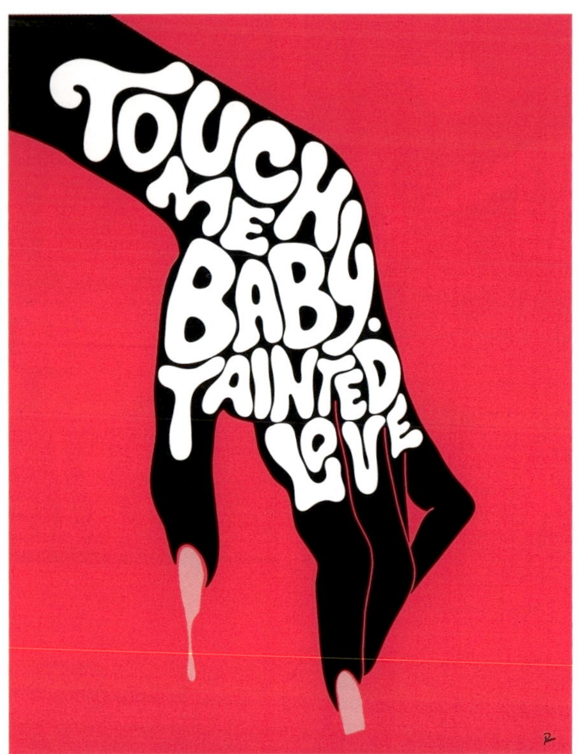

"with practically all my projects, I hand-draw the type [...] It comes more naturally to me, and for the layout it gives me a lot of freedom to play with different faces and sizes, and to make the whole really look like an image in its own right."

For the first issue of *code* magazine (autumn/winter), Parra dissociated his animal character and the text. Through the pages, a single facetious and rounded spirit makes itself at home among the teen-girl poses.

Run →

name: **Guillaume Renard**

age: **29**

workscope: **illustration, graffiti**

city: **Lille**

website: **www.777run.com**

The path travelled by illustrator Run began with conventional art-school training, then a national plastic arts diploma. But he soon became known for his trashy, baroque universe. His style, with its angular traits and rippling muscles, veers between manga and a Tim Burton aesthetic, and is heightened by gothic typography and a serious creative overflow. The pros didn't miss a trick: he was hired by *Max* magazine, then Swatch, Warner Music, Com8 and others. After creative-directing design agency Teamchman until 2003, Run is now part of the Semper FI collective, where he develops his own projects such as his *Mutafukaz* comic strip, a prizewinner at the 2003 Sundance Festival and still in search of a publisher.

The world of Mutafukaz *is a mix of 1960s sci-fi and contemporary ingredients such as hip-hop and other modern references, which make it an original product. The mood is dark and paranoid, but always tongue-in-cheek and fun,* he explains. Run, who's also inspired by Stephen Shore's minimalist photographs, the morbid sculptures of Liz McGrath, and drawings of 1960s pin-ups, is keen not to be pigeon-holed – and, even though his output is nourished by urban myths and hip-hop culture, it remains highly eclectic: *I have a natural tendency to do trash stuff, but I also know about and love doing cuter work… I adore painting watercolours, for example, and I'd really love to do children's books. In fact, that's why I recently started a 'Cute' section on my site, to show web users that there's more to my world than gothic type.* For some time now, Run has been taking part in projects outside France, in Los Angeles and Tokyo; it's a way for him to make his talent available to those who can recognise it – and an extra opportunity to explore fresh horizons.

1. "Ríos Rosas & Palm Hill neighborhood". character research for the *Mutafukaz* comic-strip project.

2. "that's amore", illustration issue of *mutafukaz* comic.
3. team angola self-portrait, for the book *football heroes*, jerzovskaja grafik + verlag / zurich (publication date: may 2006).
4. *mutafukaz* comic-strip project.

5. Illustration for *the semi permanent book 04*, design is kinky, australia.

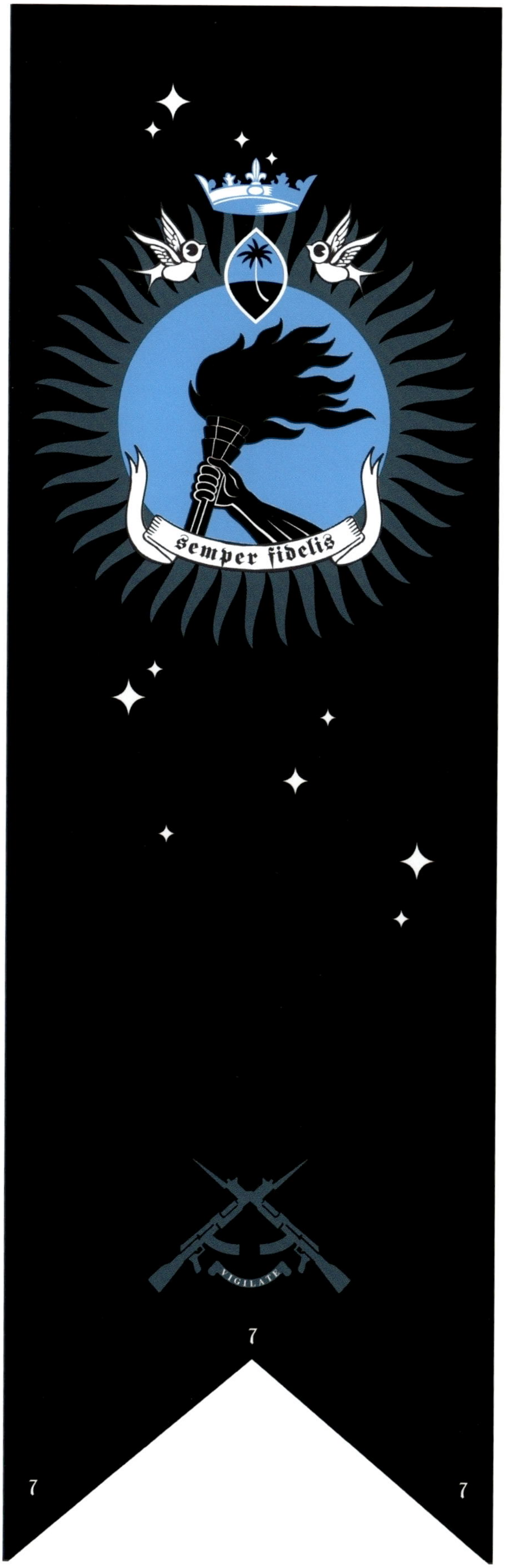

6

7

8

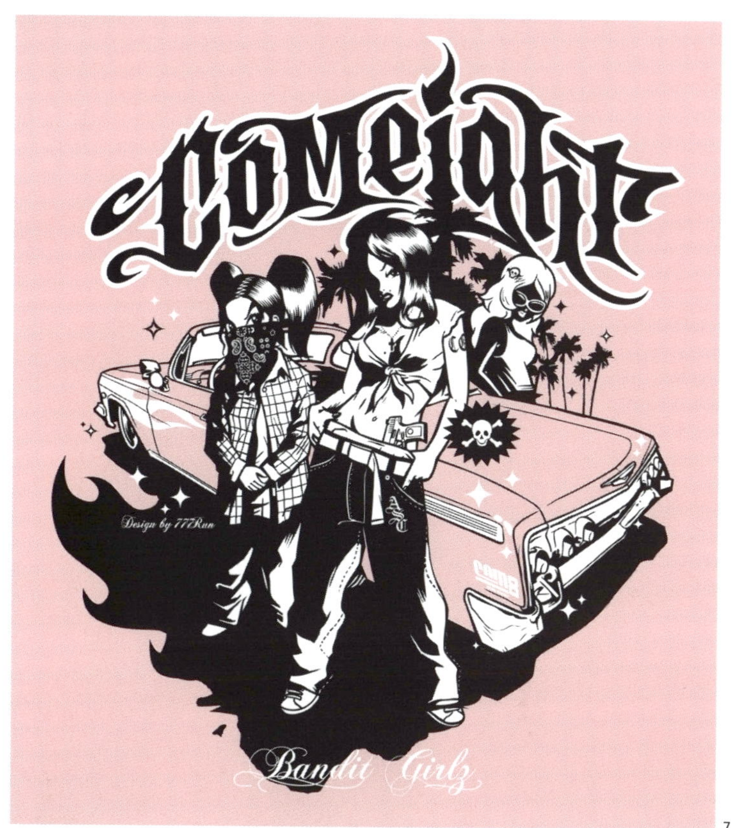

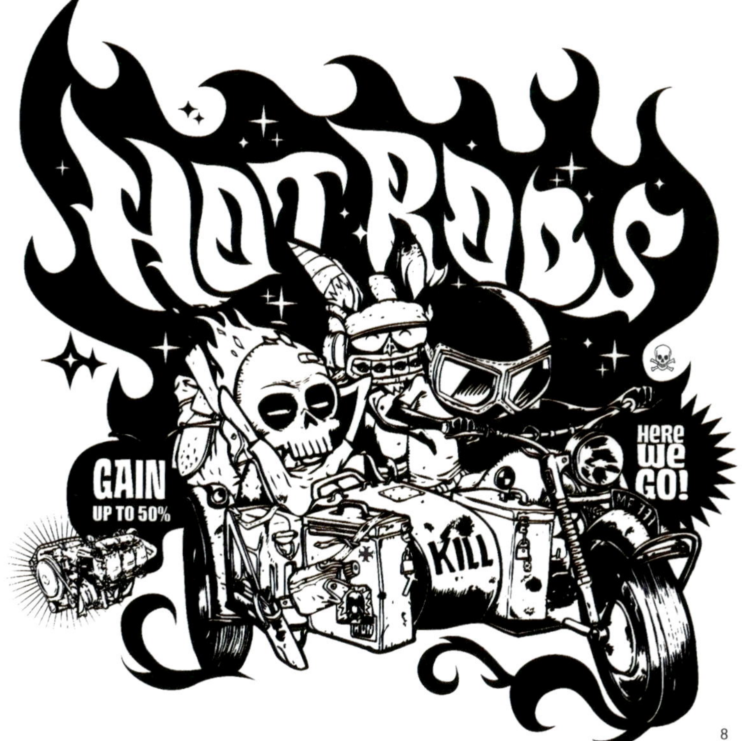

6. warrior banner by RUN / semper FI, on canvas, 80 cm x 250 cm.
7. T-shirt motif for the com8 brand (release: summer 2006).
8. "HOT RODS" issue of *Mutafukaz* comic.

start Making sense

тalking неads and now solo singer David вyrne once studied graphic design. véronique vienne unravels his **relationship with imagery**, and follows the creative thread of the covers, clips and books made by тibor кalman, sagmeister and… вyrne himself **by véronique vienne**

Much has been written about the relationship between imagery and words, but less about that between imagery and sound. And this relationship is the central concern of David Byrne, ex-leader of Talking Heads. He started making music while studying graphic design at the Rhode Island School of Design and the Maryland Institute of College of Art. The two disciplines have since fed equally into his career. He sometimes mixes his areas of interest – art-directing his discs and clips to influence how his music is positioned – but generally pursues his visual explorations separately. Trying to separate hearing and sight is instinctive. Our tendency to close our eyes to better listen to a piece of music proves that ears

"superego, ecstasy" (1997), a plastic effigy of David вyrne that expresses various emotions. іt appears on the *Feelings* album cover, designed by sagmeister, and in the "superego" project, in conjunction with powerful symbolic contexts.

perceive images as a threat. Seeing, it seems, is detrimental to listening – or, at least, depletes the acoustic experience. Any visual activity competes with the desire to hear. But any musician, whether they like it or not, relies on the images they project into the minds of their audience. This is peculiar to our era. Nowadays, the visual is used to enhance the brand image of musicians and to strengthen their affiliation with a given genre. Throughout his career, David Byrne has tried to avoid this sensory crossover in order to preserve the purity of the listening experience, but also to extricate himself from the media stranglehold that imagery exerts. His intentions, no matter how noble, have remained just that. Despite his efforts, his music has been polluted by his artistic training. He first ran up against a personal contradiction. Although

a singer of great emotional power, he has sought to present himself to his public as an intellectual. A great fan of conceptual art, he has projected onto his music oeuvre his taste for the equivocal, at odds with the personality of his voice and the character of his music. The graphics he has chosen for his discs, as well as the multiple manifestations of his visual talent – whether in books, documentaries, films, exhibitions or lectures – call to mind the existential chin-rubbing of the contemporary art world rather than the jubilant fervour that infuses his music. In 1983, with *Speaking in Tongues*, Byrne's intention was to familiarise people with world music, considered at the time to be strictly for ethnic audiences. *The idea was to present our music not as exotic, and therefore foreign, but as pop-rock that you could listen to in your car or while slouched on a sofa*, he explains. He asked Robert Rauschenberg to create the record cover and make it an atypical object, unrelated to its musical content. The result, a geometric composition incorporating a transparent plastic disc, referred to Byrne's graphic sensibility but revealed nothing about his music.

At the time, naively, we didn't want a media image. But you can't get away from it. Avoiding labels is in itself a label. I had to face facts: these days, it's impossible for a musician to travel without any visual baggage. David Byrne would like to have been a musician a hundred years ago, when, before people bought a score, they asked the in-store pianist to play the piece. Or even 70 years ago, when the first radio stations looked like musical instruments, to give people the impression they were

1.

2.

3.

4.

5.

6.

1. *speaking in tongues* (Talking Heads, 1983): a hybridisation of a primitivist painting, a photo Byrne took in a hotel, and a ramshackle typeface by Tibor Kalman. By M & Co, Kalman's studio.

2. *Little creatures* (TH, 1985): a painting by the Reverend Howard Finster. For the back visual, M & Co held a shoot to photograph the band wearing flowery suits. M. & Co.

3. *Remain in Light* (TH, 1980): the band's name in constructivist lettering. It tops the portraits of the four former design students. The primitive masks are actually a stage in the processing of the image by a software program experimented with at the Massachusetts Institute of Technology. The band has more recently used scientific imaging. M. & Co.

4. "Naked" (TH, 1988): Considering America to be too self-absorbed, the band recorded the album in Paris with musicians of different artistic and geographic origins. The cover, from a concept by David Byrne, questions the audience about their roots. M. & Co.

5. Produced with Brian Eno (Talking Heads' producer), *My Life in the Bush of Ghosts* (1981) was all about experimentation: after recording sounds in Africa, the duo mixed them and played with musicians over the rhythms thus generated. The voices are samples from discs of pop music, speeches by politicians, and TV-evangelist sermons. The visual is from a video work by Eno, and the ultra-neutral type is credited to… Peter Saville.

6. *uh-oh* (David Byrne, 1991) blends genres: olde Englishe type, painting by Brian Dewan, drawing by David Byrne. M. & Co. In their clips and

concerts, Talking Heads seek to elude the representational idioms of our time. Directed by Tibor Kalman, the video for "(Nothing but) Flowers" required fastidious typographic work, interweaving the lyrics with sociological statistics.

attending a concert rather than a broadcast. But now, listeners also consume images. They have to be given something to look at, to support their aural attention. iPod users don't listen with their eyes closed. Music is the soundtrack that turns everyday life into a constant spectacle. In 1984, Talking Heads accidentally came across a visual that suited them, and which to this day has remained the emblem of their music. *Where's your big suit?* fans still ask David Byrne when they spot him in the street. The big suit was Byrne's stage outfit, an outsize number immortalised in the documentary *Stop Making Sense* and on the cover of the album of the same name. Byrne's original intention was to subvert a symbol – that of corporate culture – and appropriate it to show that even highly conventional people are actually very cool. The

irony of the big suit was that, in the end, the subversion was subverted and became the band's brand image. All of a sudden, Byrne's peculiar garb was part of his music. In *True Stories*, a sardonic film he directed in 1986, he wore another suit, that of a Texan urban cowboy, a disguise quite as laughable as his gigantic business suit (this was at a time when Americans could openly poke fun at Texas without the fear of being branded unpatriotic). But these displays of derision, which enthralled his fans, were only a camouflage that hid the emotional dimension of his music and the moving inflections of his voice: *"the voice of a little boy lost at the zoo"* (Village Voice); *"he sings like Tony Perkins would have sung if Psycho had been a musical"* (Rolling Stone). Byrne himself, caught up in the parody game, didn't realise that his eccentricities masked

the originality of his talent. *My songs* [from the time of Talking Heads] *had an emotional resonance that people found disturbing, and I didn't fully appreciate this*, he says now. After pondering the issue, he admits that he sings to tap his emotions. In his most recent CD, *Grown Backward*, he allows himself his first love song – a Verdi aria, "Un di Felice", from *La Traviata* – and provides his own violin and cello accom-paniment. His previously latent affectivity was hidden by the über-quirky character he projected on stage. Commentators went to town describing his *"neurotic evangelist's approach [...] his teen awkwardness, [...] his post-electric-shock appearance, or even his bemused air – like someone who's just spent half an hour on rinse cycle in a washing machine"*. Amazingly devoid of personal coquetry, David Byrne never seems at ease. He has

ABOVE. A piece of TV counter-culture, "Love for sale" borrows advertising clichés and subjects marketed musicians to all the treatments normally reserved for FMCGS: panning shot, chocolate sauce, packaging…

BELOW. *stop making sense*, the concert filmed by director JONATHAN DEMME, and which thanks to him acquired the status of a film in its own right. Instead of the usual scenic effects – lighting, dance, etc. – the band, led by BYRNE, came up with other bits of stage business: jogging, setting up the instruments while BYRNE played, with rhythm accompaniment provided by a single cassette player, and… the big suit.

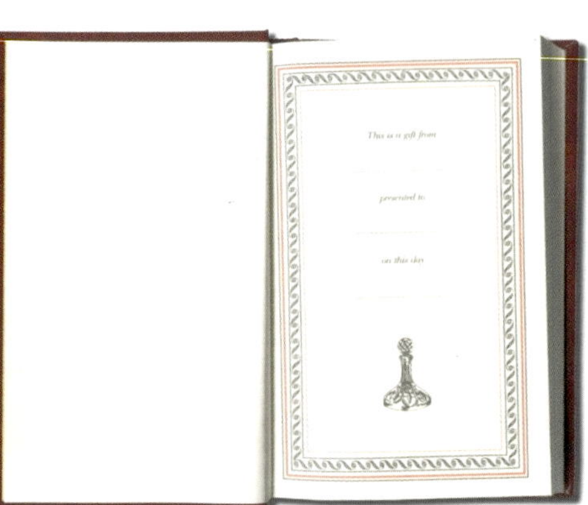

no taste for mawkishness, and intellectualises his feelings to distance himself from them. *We'd do well to systematically distrust all that's sweet and gentle*, he writes in his ironical little bible *The New Sins*.
This same sense of unease pervades his films, videos, conceptual artworks and CD covers. In 1997, he even stretched the irony and created a plastic figurine in his image, a homunculus that he features, *à la* Cindy Sherman, in a series of pseudo-realistic photomontages. Some of the shots were subsequently used in an odd booklet, *Your Action World*, an ersatz corporate gift in a plasticised cover – an epigrammatic item that he made with Stefan Sagmeister.

The central theme of Byrne's graphic œuvre is his critique of corporate culture, which he parodies unrelentingly; he's ready to

enjoy a laugh, but also to amaze himself. His main worktool is his camera, with which he takes pictures of empty conference rooms, corporate signage, office items, platforms, corridors, hoardings, merchandise being unwrapped at trade fairs, deserted hotel rooms, and aircraft interiors. Minimalist and offbeat, these images may find their way into exhibitions, art galleries, or books intended for limited readerships. His most ambitious and original achievement has been a small art film released in 2004, made from PowerPoint images. Initially devised as a parody – Byrne's favourite approach – the project soon took an engrossing turn. The Microsoft application, which is supposed to offer "ready-to-click" graphic solutions, gradually revealed a wacky iconographic world which Byrne exploited to create an

abstract animated cartoon – with a musical soundtrack, of course – featuring a succession of barley sugar-coloured arabesques, loony diagrams, image-eating typefaces and lacy graphic exercises that languorously drape the screen. A primitive spectacle that in no way rivals the special effects we are all used to. And yet the film, released in DVD format with the title *Envisioning Emotional Epistemological Information* (in tribute to Edward Tufte) is curiously affecting. A systematic exploration of his website (davidbyrne.com) lays bare the singer-guitarist's many fields of interest and his eclectic inquisitiveness. The links include a site dedicated to the painting elephants of Thailand, and that of publisher McSweeney's, run by Dave Eggers, author of the bestseller *A Heartbreaking Work of Staggering Genius*. But perhaps the most

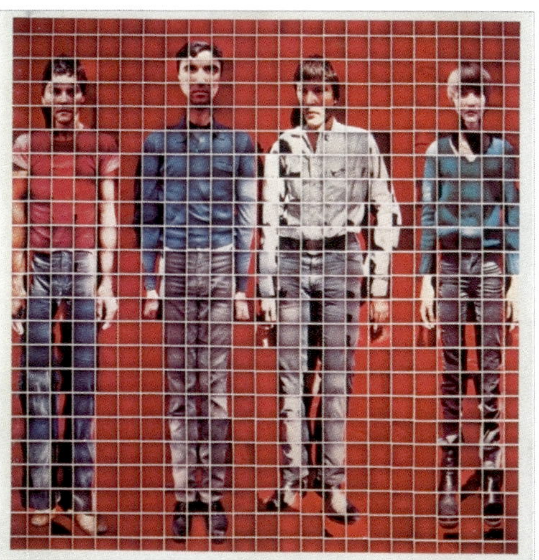

DAVID BYRNE designed the covers of TALKING HEADS' first albums: *77* (1977), *More Songs About Building & Food* (1978) (this page)… and, with DANIELLE SPENCER, those of his most recent discs, *Lead Us Not Into Temptation* (2003) and *Grown Backward* (2004) (facing page).

PHOTO-novel made up of image-bank photos, published in *Your Action world*.

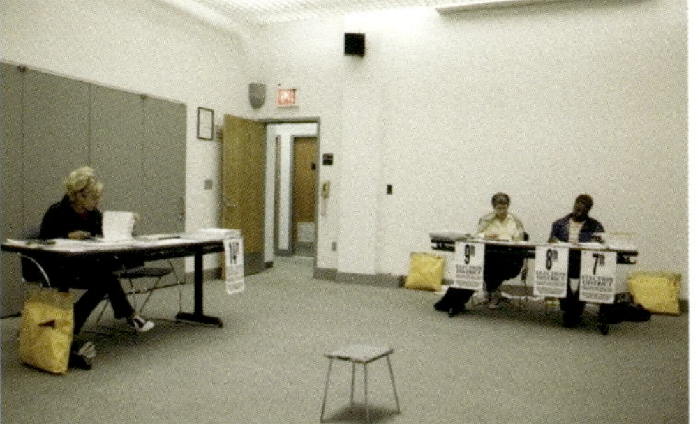

Itsy-Bitsy Democracy / Big Fucking Democracy (2004). Installation by DAVID BYRNE and DANIELLE SPENCER, showing how democracy can appear insignificant or imposing. http://a.parsons.edu/~voting_booth/

with Danielle Spencer, Byrne did a piece on corporate signage at Research Triangle Park, North Carolina. The logos were photographed and then invested with other content in imperative mode: believe, etc.

"Better Living Through Chemistry", a series of images plagiarising advertising letterwork. It blends motivational slogans with bank photos and drug-use utensils. Shown on 3m x 4m hoardings and in your Action world.

Designed by Stefan Sagmeister in the style of an annual report, *your action world* explores and challenges the communication business: photo-novel made from image banks, flat blocks of brand colours, photos of hotel rooms, and images from his previous work.

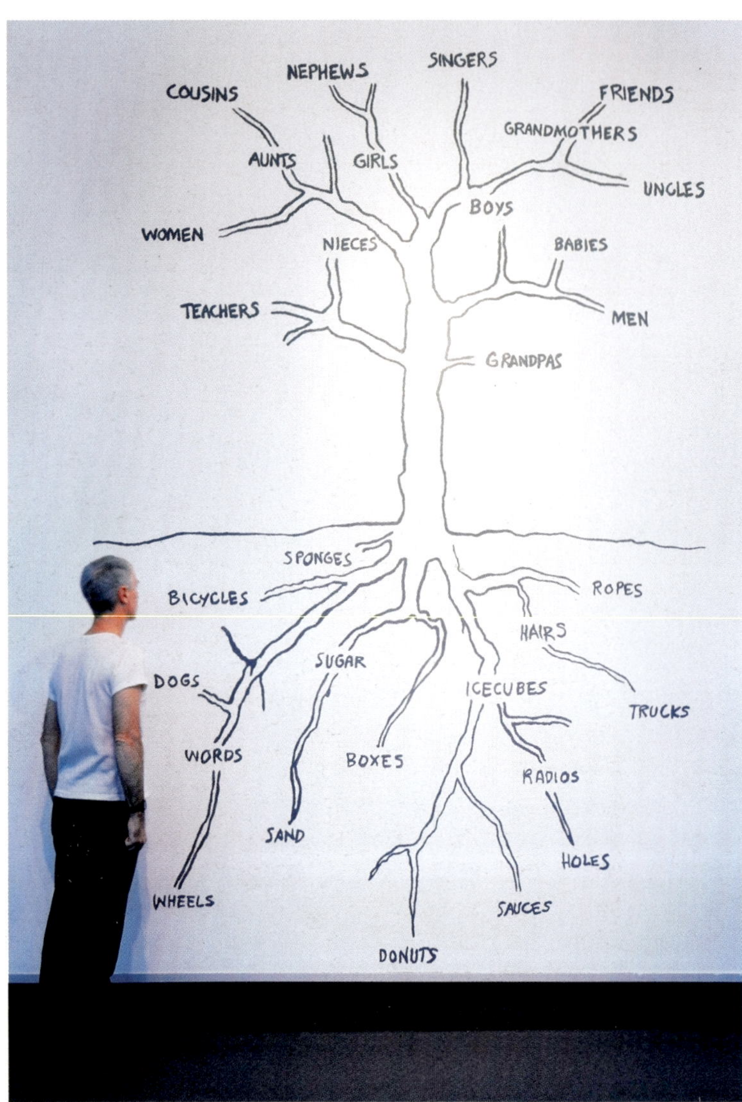

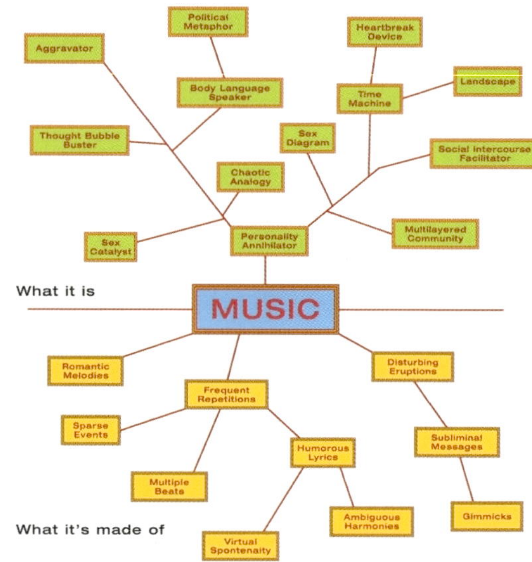

Left. "Tree drawings". Diagrams that prefer the uncertainty of organic form explore the roots and fruits of contemporary phenomena. *What is It?*, Southeastern Center for Contemporary Art, Winston-Salem (2003); and *Music: What It Is and What It's Made of* (2002).

Facing page (top). *Playing the Building.* David Byrne's building organ is a wind instrument: its sounds are created by the piping and percussion / vibrations of the entire building structure.

Facing page (bottom). *EEEI* (Envisioning Emotional Epistemological Information). The PowerPoint software program explored as a mode of artistic expression, to make images and a film. As with many of Byrne's projects, art creates a tension in everyday visual languages, revealing their limits and orientations.

eye-popping section of Byrne's site is his diary, a blog describing what goes through his head daily, and where he posts his latest photos and visual brainwaves. To appreciate David Byrne's talent thus requires a dual personality – musical on one side, visual on the other. As much graphic artist as musician (and that's from the horse's mouth), the ex-leader of Talking Heads now divides his time between his two careers: conceptual visual artist and stage virtuoso. Still better known for his music than for his installations, he blends the two genres – on one hand creating eerie or wacky visuals for his CDs, which hurts his popularity among the general public, and on the other hand leveraging his tremendous reputation as a musician to convey his artistic projects to the press, though without attaining legitimacy in the world of contemporary art.

This article is indeed an example of the impossible predicament in which David Byrne puts himself (and us) by pursuing two passions at once. His graphic work can only be critiqued in the context of his musical development, and vice versa. But our dilemma does not interest him. He is too busy: half a dozen projects are in progress in his Soho, New York studio, a place dedicated to visual creation, far from the musical activities he carries out separately, at home. In his most recent piece, staged in Stockholm, he converted a loft into a huge musical instrument, connecting the building's metal structure and piping to a small electronic organ, so he could make the whole building vibrate and play tunes that resounded with terrifying strangeness. Far too involved with his many centres of interest to talk about them, David Byrne refuses

any interview seeking to present him as a musician who "does art". Yet this highly talented guitarist is delighted when described as a conceptual artist with more than one string to his instrument.

OUT OF TOUCH
DAZED AND CONFUSED
ANGRY AND VIOLENT
TRIED ONCE BEFORE
BRAVE AND TRUE
DANGEROUS WHEN CORNERED
HOMELESS
CONSIDERATE AND KIND

monsters__R__us

Every era has its own monsters – they're a sign of the cultural and **aesthetic times**. spawned by artists or by the collective unconscious, these **creatures** are the sometimes moral reflection of our apprehensions and aberrations **by vanina pinter**

Over the centuries, our repertoire of monsters has grown ever richer, and we have been keen to classify them in families, as necessary creatures of the imagination. In this field, Greek mythology is still a top-drawer source.[1]

Christianity moved away from pagan fantasy (though it has had its gargoyles and other excesses, lurking in the tympanums) to stigmatise shameful behaviour (we shudder with horror or grin bawdily at the paintings of Bosch and Goya). The 19th century, with its faith in rationalism and technology, created the first monsters of science fiction: machine-monsters hatched by scientists themselves. But in the genre's history, the last century was without doubt the most decisive: monsters of immorality, dictators, 'sacred monsters' (with the star system), scary robots, and genetic abnormality…

The 21st century dawned amid resounding success for disaster scenarios and heroes juggling reality and the paranormal – to such a point that monsters of every ilk are now part and parcel of our everyday life. But – and here's where the new millennium bucks the trend – they no longer really scare us! The monster and the cuddly toy sometimes cross over to engender a single being: many toys with monster-like grins are more cuddly than anything,[2] yet they cut themselves off from the world of childhood with their harshness and violence, which are all the more conspicuous since child-beating and paedophilia are no longer passed over in silence. The shift towards the spectacular is coupled with the feeling that we need to grow up a little and look tricky subjects in the eye.

1. The world of Tomer Hanuka is pitiless. Its harshness and human violence is reflected in characters' faces; they too are on the borderline between monstrousness and degenerate humanity. www.thanuka.com

2. The monsters of Japanese Taro Niijima are iconographically conventional (dragons, etc.), but contemporary in their (electronic and industrial) components.
www.nwba-japan.com/artists/taro_niijima

3. A Fabrica resident, François Prost has built black and white robots, collated from bits of a thousand everyday items. These composite monsters also echo the mandalas drawn by Geneviève Gauckler and the figures of London studio Insect.
www.g2works.com
www.insect.co.uk

4.5.6.7. Appealing monsters, very ugly but very cute. A family spirit links the current generation of monsters, which have a clear affiliation with cuddly and other toys. In Lille, France, skwak (4.6), www.skwak.free.fr, does canvases of monsters and toys. In Toronto, Canadian Nicholas Di Genova (7), www.mediumphobic.com, goes for super-sharp linework, but with pastel

hues; meanwhile Koa (5), www.koadzn.com, has a penchant for silly beasties and, together with Lazy Dog, has even published *War of Monstars*, a graphic battle with contributions from graphic artists, illustrators and graffers from around the world: Baseman, Burgerman, Hydro74 and others.

In a brighter-eyed, bushier-tailed vein, the Pictoplasma generation[3] is surrounding itself with a host of creatures straight out of fairy tales (cuddly toys and Playmobil-style robots), a small army that can perform various functions: reassure, be personalised, talk about their personal mythologies, and give free rein to the imagination… The phenomenon is far from marginal, and gathering pace in both specialist shops and high-end outlets. The fashion world is conjuring monsters too (Christian Lacroix has designed a whole series), scrambling the traditional grammar of the genre, while also combining craftsmanship and luxury at the same level.
In addition to these bits of plastic and fabric are a clutch of junk monsters, illustrated here: conglomerations of detritus, the symbols of our consumerist excesses and a soul-searching eco-society… these garbage hybrids are put together with a virtuoso flair that's often fascinating.
Ultimately, it seems fairly odd that our society, so fearful of latent terrorism and uncertain tomorrows, has such gentle monsters. It's noteworthy that all of them, like toys, have virtues and appearances akin to good-luck charms and voodoo statuettes – which are also being marketed with great success. The attraction can also be explained by our current neo-baroque mood, avid for arabesques and ornamental linework – and thus for grotesques and all manner of imaginary figures, weird and decorative. But these monsters' benevolence is also due to their software genes: Photoshop

WAR
CIRCUS
HELP
HOT
MORE RISK
MY BRAIN IS IN MY FEET
CANDY MANIAC
INFECTED
YOU ARE SO CUTE
BEAUTIFUL
HAPPY BIRTHDAY
I'M HAPPY
JUST TO SAY HELLO
LOVE
EVIL IS HERE
U ARE USELESS
I HATE ANIMALS
I KNOW
FEED THE MONSTER
DEATH
DESTROY
ALL THE CHILDREN WANT TO BE A MANIAC
I KNOW WHO YOU ARE
STOP
EAT
I LOVE ICE CREAM
ONCE UPON A TIME
NO
KILL HUMANS
PLUSH POWA
FEAR
LOVE
WE LOVE YOU
YOU KILL MY SON
I WANT TO FUCK YOU
BUT I'VE LOST MEGA DICK
WHERE I AM?
DON'T FORGET WHO WE ARE
EAT
KILL
KOOGAI
NO!!
Pollute Me
OH
SKWAK

4

5

MANIAC SORCERER
ATTACK! KOOGAI!
SKWAK

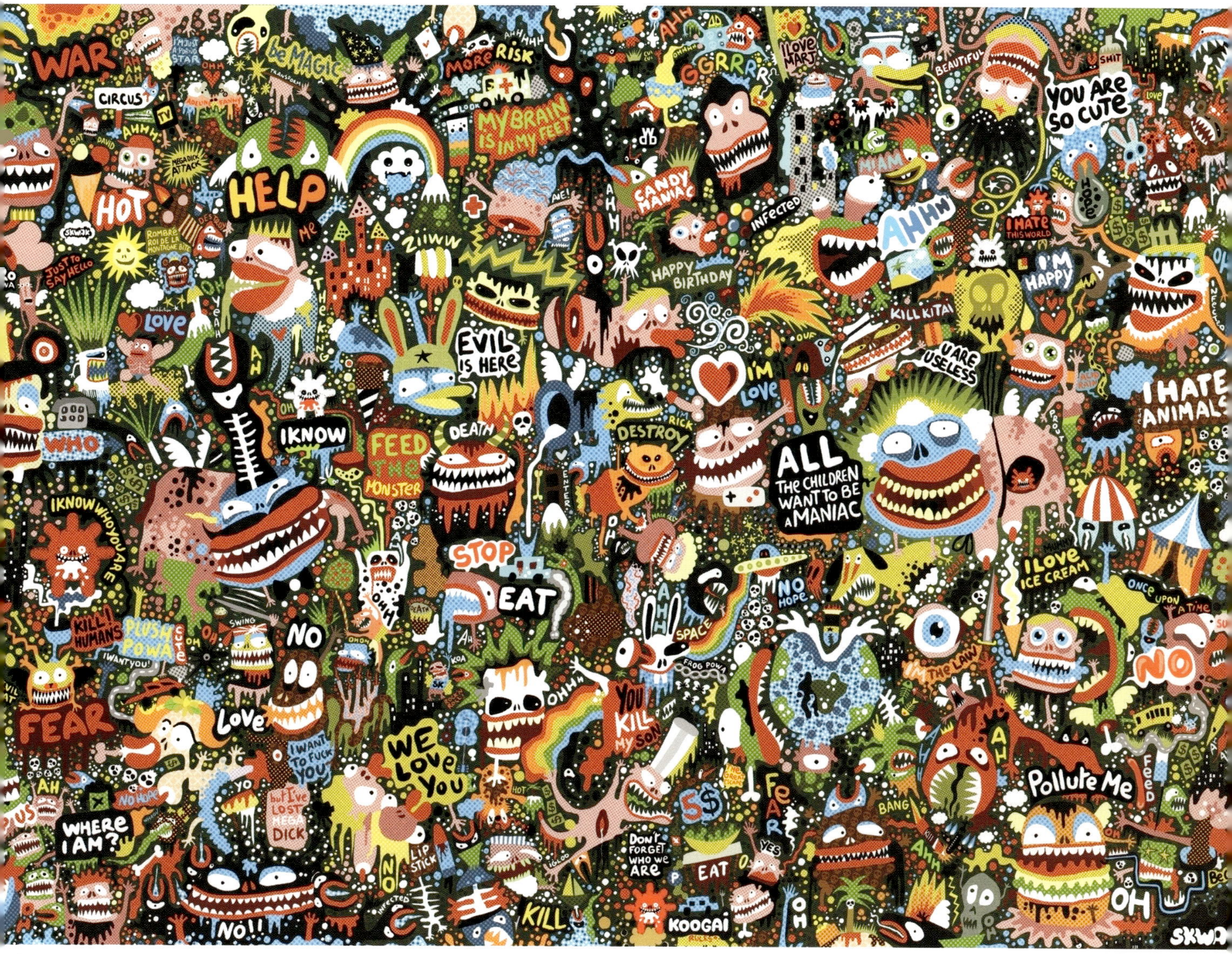

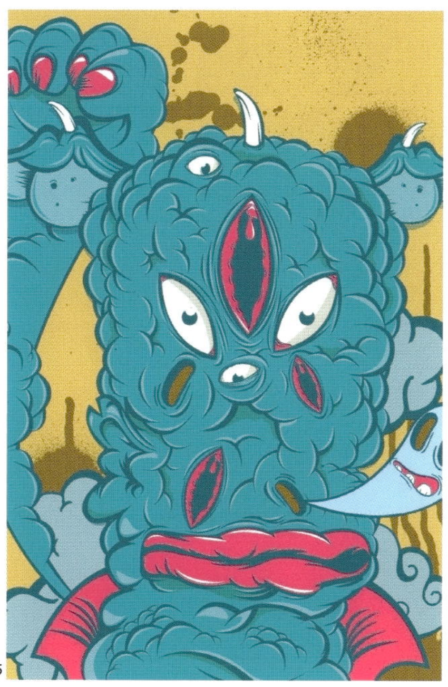

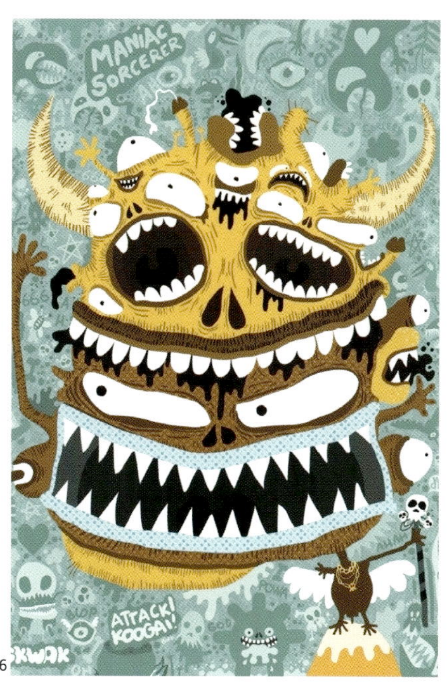

6

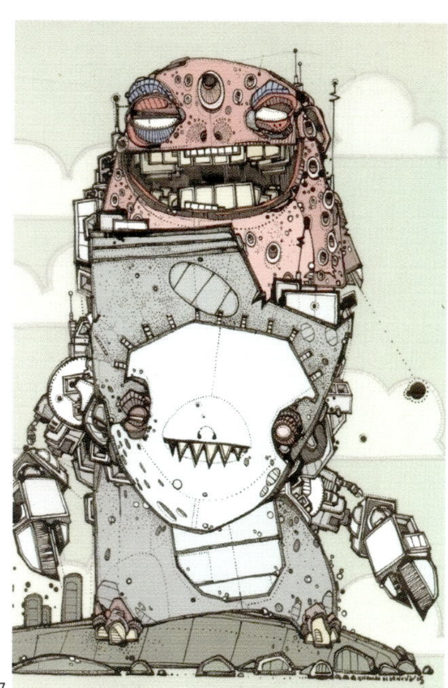

7

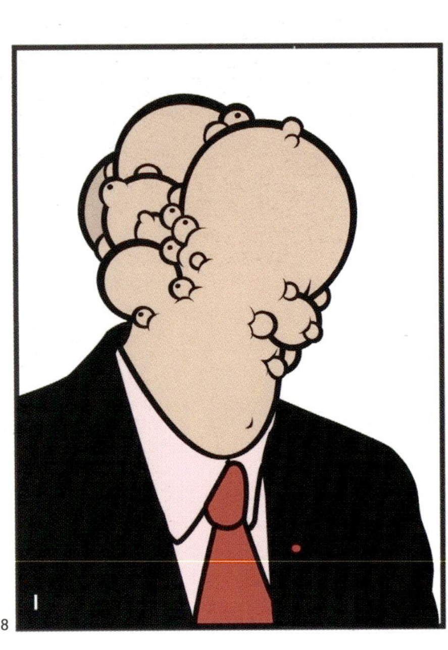

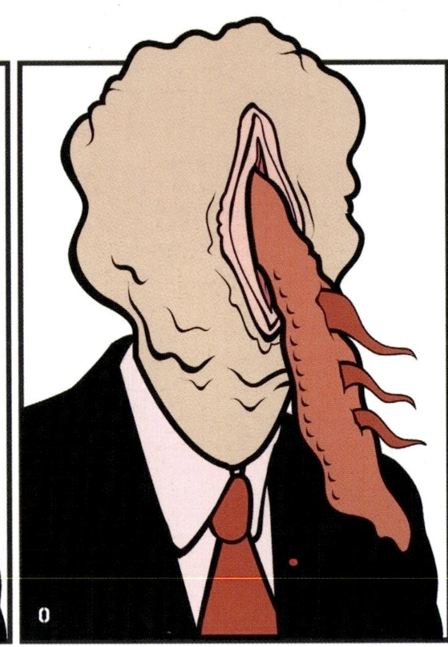

8

8. In the view of Lille-based studio Incorect, monsterland – and here they claim kinship with Loulou Picasso – is a place for political incorrectness and critical, non-conformist outbursts of our surroundings. Here, a piece by studio member Izo. www.incorect.com

9. Ryohei Tanaka, a Japanese who splits his time between art and caring for mentally disabled children, has caught the eye with his perfectly symmetrical paper cut-outs, and is now starting to use colour.

10. Young Turk Gokhan Okur (born 1981) has been self-employed for five years. "My monsters are part of me. They're self-portraits of suffering, with tortured minds."
www.kofti.com

11. Motomichi Nakamura has always injected spattered blood, humour and scarlet mucus in his black-and-white Flash animations. His creatures are now sometimes the sole subject of his paintings. When animated, they are even more ferocious. Their graphic simplicity hides the cruelty.
www.motomichi.com

9

10

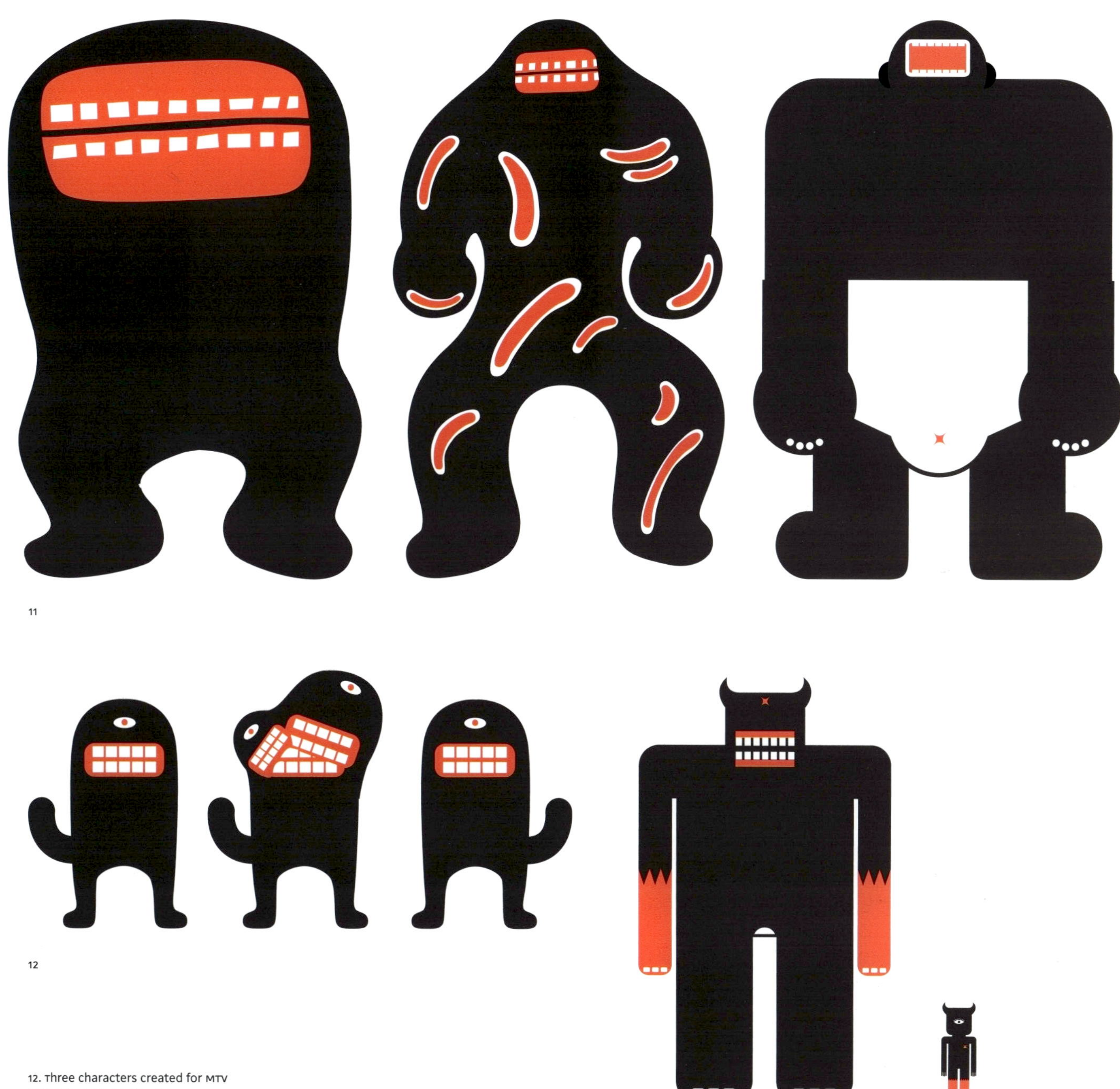

12. Three characters created for MTV
online by Motomichi Nakamura.

promotes slickly realistic photomontages, while Illustrator, with its clean round contours, bright colours and flat-block surfaces, produces a mellow tone.

There is, however, some reassuring cheer. The scarily dreadful reflections of our fears and of our latent and contemptible impulses endure – in the form of other monsters we prefer not to look at and which often have human features (toys tend to have bestial faces), descendents of mangas and of the punk generations of Bazooka and Charles Burns... whose violent streak is untempered. Here the linestyle, with its hand-drawn residue, is more acute and jerky, roughing up humans so they understand they are incomprehensible monsters.[4]

1. Think of minotaurs, mermaids, chimeras, medusas, dragons, cerberuses, sphinxes...
2. The world of Walt Disney and the film Monsters, Inc.
3. For the past few years Berlin event Pictoplasma, including talks and exhibitions, has been attracting a whole generation of graphic designers and graffiti artists who switch happily between illustration and the design of 3D figurines. www.pictoplasma.com. Various Pictoplasma books have been published by Die Gestalten Verlag.
4. From Blaise Pascal's Pensées.

Absolutely
fabrica?

opened in 1994 in Italy, the **communication** research centre of holding company Edizione experiments with a **hybrid** kind of **training**. Young graduates spend a year getting to grips with the **graphic-design** marketplace and with Benetton, their **patron/employer** by vanina pinter

Deep in Venetia, one of Italy's most dynamic regions, Fabrica, Benetton's centre for communication research – an emblem of triumphant capitalist Italy – is an isolated fortress located near Treviso, living a life of near self-sufficiency. Its stakeholders state that Fabrica does not think in Italian: *we are a republic in the heart of Italy*. The parent company, like its laboratory, is a multinational; and the participants – the supervisory team and guest artists – come from all over the world. The 'students' readily liken the place to a luxurious cosmopolitan inn, where camaraderie is coupled with the stringent standards and mindset of serious professionals. Eleven years into its existence, this mini-state, where English is the working language, is flourishing.

Trying to tell

From the outside, defining Fabrica – how it works, its spirit and commitments – turns out to be a tricky task. From a French standpoint, a school that gets into bed with a profit-making enterprise immediately looks dubious. But once you're actually there, the creative and individualistic components fit seamlessly together. Renzo di Renzo, Fabrica's creative director (he took over from Oliviero Toscani and his 'dictatorship' six years ago), explains: *It's hard to define what Fabrica is, especially as it's one of a kind and the place is in a state of constant flux. We're creating and paving the way at the same time. We build everything with the aim of adapting to shifting market situations. Our model is something between the Bauhaus and Andy Warhol's Factory*. Fabrica is not an agency or a school. There are no classes, just workshops lasting a few days. And lectures are held every month with established stars and young, up-and-coming figures. The students are selected by application and tested for a week (or longer, depending on the subject: video students have three weeks to make a film, after which they're in or out). There's one compulsory condition: be aged under 25. Fifty students join Fabrica for one year – they receive board,

views from the Fabrica atrium and staircase. Tadao Ando's architecture combines concrete and the zen spirit, playing on emptiness and emphatic lines.

students and supervisors in the
industrial design department.

lodging and a bursary – but they arrive all round the year; there's no official start of term. There's a constant flow: some arrive in May, others leave in December, and during this time they can travel to execute commissions. They have to operate in three areas: work specific to Benetton (website, video animations, stores, etc.), for external clients (generally non-profit organisations that seek support from Fabrica) and their own projects (sometimes, these turn into Benetton tools, credited to the creative and disseminated in all countries[1]). How are people chosen? *We look for people with no preconceptions, who recognise diversity. Before, under Toscani, the place created disciples. We don't want to make clones any more, we want to help individuals thrive. And another point: technical knowledge is not the most important thing.*

Multidisciplinary

By its very architecture, the place promotes a cross-discipline approach. Japanese architect Tadao Ando has added to the previous old building a contemporary wing – a piece of sub-surface architecture whose walls are large bay windows opening onto a round atrium. A fairly cold, zen-like air fills the deserted premises. But the rooms are always open, and the photography and visual communication areas are open-plan spaces conducive to popping in and out and meeting people. Most projects require expertise from at least two disciplines; students frequently find they have affinities with one of their peers, with whom they work on personal projects. During their residency, they each have an office and computer. Heavy equipment (dark room, recording studio, etc.) are at their disposal. At present there are seven departments: photography, Web & interactivity, industrial design (the former fashion department has now been folded into this department), video & film, music, and visual communication... and a creative writing department, set up two years ago and geared equally to scripts, short stories and reportage. In their internal operation, the departments are multi-

Above. Two images from the Diversity project, 2005. For the second world PR Festival, dedicated to the theme of diversity, students created images that were gathered into a booklet and on a website: www.worldprfestival.org. Left, photo by Matthew Haigh. Right, illustration by Nicole Kenney.

Below. Young graphic designer Andy Rementer started off with illustrations done in his sketchbook in order to create the poster, illustrations and logo – the whole identity, in fact – for "Teach me", a four-day lecture series developed by Fabrica and university Iuav of Venice (staged in late September 2005).

Above. Last issue of *colors*, a quarterly dedicated to Reporters Sans Frontières. Its art director is Renzo di Renzo: "*colors* predates Fabrica, but then we absorbed it. It's single-themed, which is its way of addressing subjects that matter. we try to say something that others don't. It raises awareness of the ties between west and east. we can say things that the organisation can't."

Right and below, both pages. In 2004, to celebrate its 10th anniversary, Fabrica published a colossal general survey, *From chaos to order and back*, featuring all the images designed by the centre.
It is entirely based on visuals: no text. In full-page format, the face-offs are explosive, and the visual treatments are both chaotic and hilarious.
Ten jackets serve as covers. Here, two of the covers and four spreads.

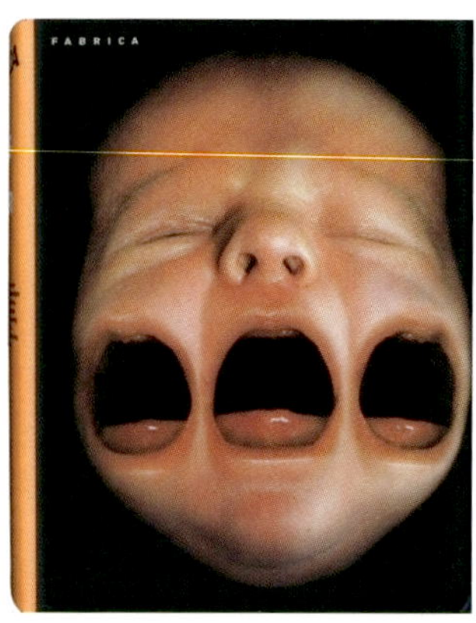

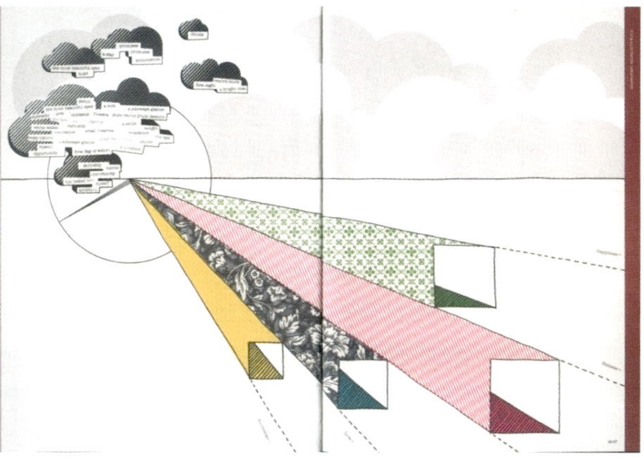

Left. Cover and spread of *FAB* magazine. This themed publication is produced entirely by the students. The first half of the magazine presents their personal ideas in writing, graphics, object design, etc. The second half presents Fabrica's activities and commissions.

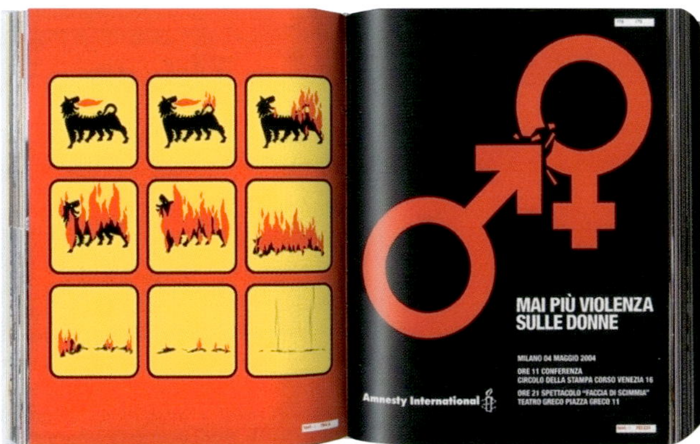

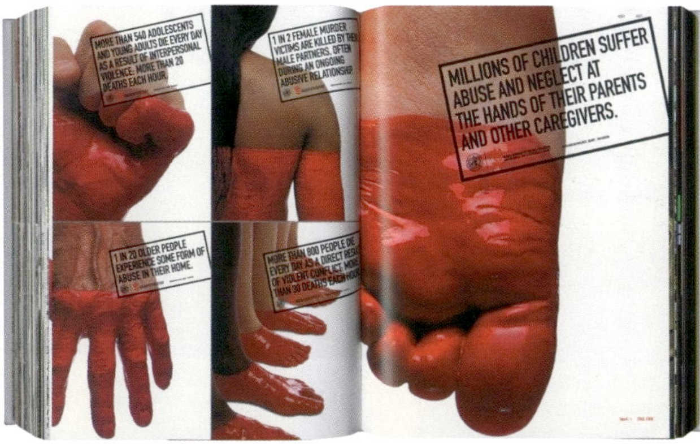

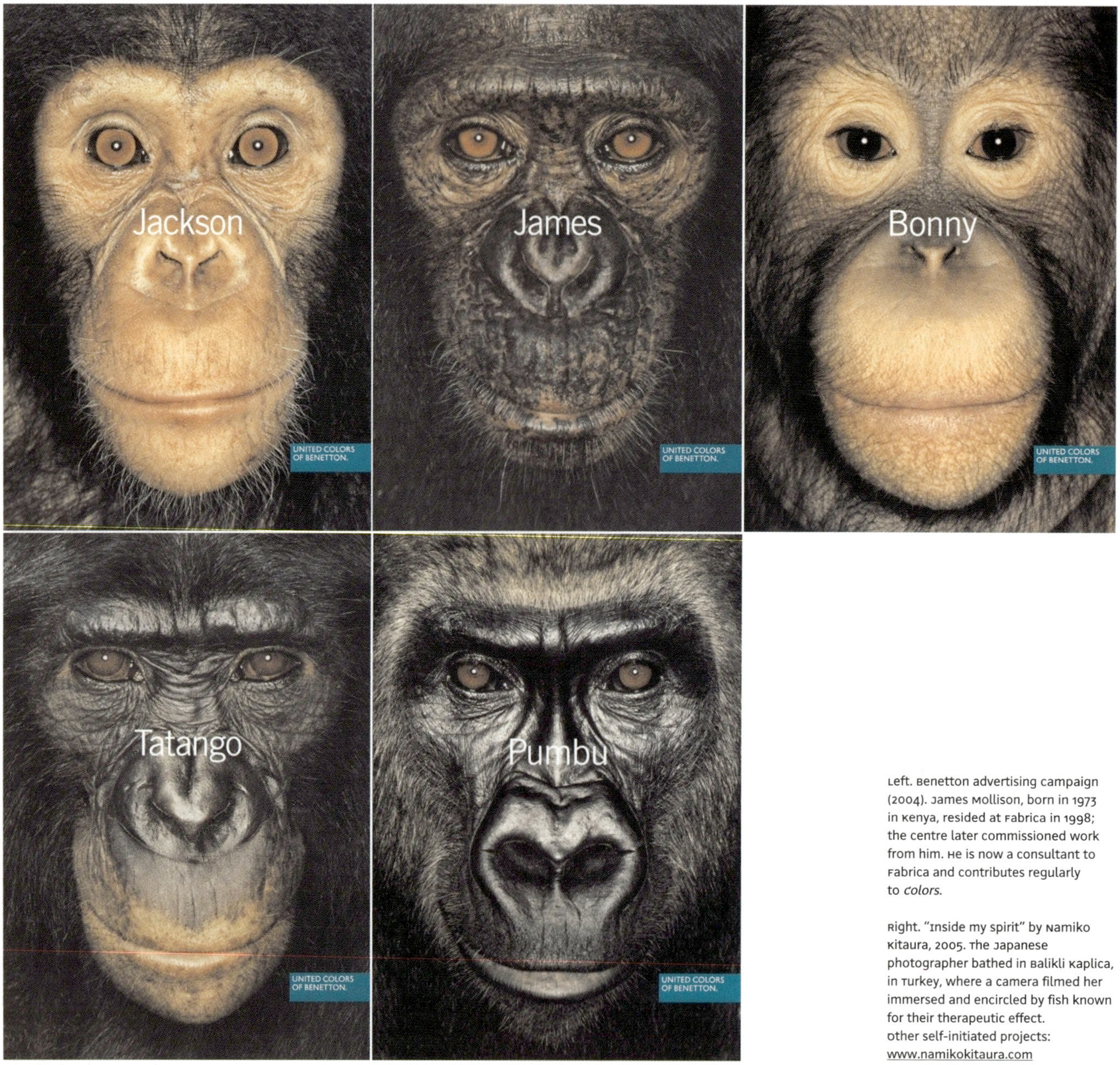

Left. Benetton advertising campaign (2004). James Mollison, born in 1973 in Kenya, resided at Fabrica in 1998; the centre later commissioned work from him. He is now a consultant to Fabrica and contributes regularly to *colors*.

Right. "Inside my spirit" by Namiko Kitaura, 2005. The Japanese photographer bathed in Balikli Kaplica, in Turkey, where a camera filmed her immersed and encircled by fish known for their therapeutic effect. Other self-initiated projects: www.namikokitaura.com

sided: video, for example, covers documentary film, animation, motion graphics and experimental testing. The system is intended to be flexible, democratic and flat-structured.

graphic commitments

Omar Vulpinari, who has headed the visual communication department (16 people including 10 students) for eight years, acknowledges that his section is closely linked with the social themes bequeathed by Benetton's background and by Toscani (they continue to work for the UN, the WHO, Reporters Sans Frontières, and so on). He has no doubt he enjoys *a privileged, ideal situation. [...] Fabrica is a unique model that spans training and business, a utopia of opportunity for young people and corporate growth. A win-win recipe. The student is paid, given a portfolio of international projects, and at the same time starts making contacts. Fabrica breathes innovation into Benetton, and the group gets the spin-offs with the public. It's a training model for the future, and all universities are starting to adopt this type of education. It's based on change and speed. We want to train young people to be flexible and attuned to what's happening around them – and that's impossible in traditional universities.* The man is convinced of his method. And it must be said that the benefits for Benetton are inestimable: 360° creativity on a thousand and one supports. For the students, it all depends on their personality. There are those who come to have a good time and discover themselves; others to knuckle down and understand the nuts and bolts of business; some use Fabrica as a springboard, where they build up an address book, as much as an exhibition interface; while others, as yet unsure of what they want, are giving themselves a gap year between graduate school and the world of work, and aren't quite sure what to think of this corporate utilitarianism. Creative personalities, meanwhile, must learn to fit the Fabrica mould. *Yes, there is a Fabrica style, our images are characterised by wordless, speechless visuals for a wide audience, designed by a global*

Above and right. "Happiness in the garden", 2005: garden items designed by Frezza for Casamania. Many items have been created, including these bird nests and outdoor shower. The clothes line is currently being produced.

Fab Features are areas attached to Benetton stores (fewer than 10 worldwide, so far). They show residents' projects and sell objects made by the young team. Here, the Fabricando notebook and two-way slippers.

source – international students. They have an archetypal character, they address universal values. They're shocking, certainly… they aim to reach as many people as possible. An emotional reaction is clearly intended. We want to be persuasive – to give audiences a punch in the eye, an explosion in the brain. At the same time, the students' personal scrapbooks suggest very diverse styles. The students are selected for their graphic language, not their style. Discussing his personal experience of Fabrica, Vulpinari says it reminds him daily that *it's important not to do graphic design for its own sake, and that you have to communicate to others, create a visual mirror, a holistic empathy.*

Leading, but followed?

Ultimately, there's no doubt that the school knows how to sell itself, play host to the curious – whether journalists or Japanese ministerial delegations – and reveal its workings. Although the model is reaping rewards, it has not yet been duplicated. But it's important not to misjudge Fabrica: it's not a school, and no training is dispensed. One wonders to what extent this lab for learning about working life – where personal talent is clearly integrated into a collective enterprise – is legitimate or poses a danger. Entrants are advised to be well-braced and savvy so they don't feel used when they leave. And one last word of warning: Fabrica's experimentation is not elitist or highly cultural; rather, it is pragmatic and jovial, with a tone that inclines towards the dramatic.

1. As with Juan Ospina's flipbook.

www.fabrica.it: the site is comprehensive, feat-uring most of the artists' work and everyone who works, and has worked, at Fabrica.

тotems and signage items guiding visitors in the рarchi de мestre at the gateway to venice, 2004.

рeversible vase, vase/saltpot and bowl: objects from the "ғab тab" collection (2005), tablewares designed for рaola с. and shown in мilan in 2005.

вelow. "cylinder" (2004), an experiment conducted by artists in the industrial design and music departments. using a software program, they can translate and give form to sounds: pieces of music, speeches, and so on.

Blason Level Art,
Mexican performance,
vectorial picture by DOB(R)MAN.

playing field **Level**

In Nantes, western France, the **Level Art collective** explores the neighbouring urban realms of graphic design (with a **graffiti** edge) and merchandising. Right now, the outfit has **eight members** and as many tendencies by Hugo van Offel

The Level Art collective was hatched after an encounter at the École d'Arts Graphiques in Nantes. Several students with graphic affinities decided to create a comics fanzine, *Level*. Even in their early days, a highly distinctive aesthetic was forming, influenced equally by comics, graphic design and advertising. After three issues of the fanzine, which met with so-so success, the 10 members of the team got the chance to publish a collection of illustrations. To do so they set up a non-profit association – and thus was Level Art born. Even then, *we had a wide range of styles. Little by little, we grew from 10 to 17 members – graphic designers, graffers and illustrators – doing their own thing.* Today Level Art has eight members,

LEVEL ART (LVL):
STROM (Romaric Dabin), aged 29, Nantes
LLOR (Laure Le Fol), 25, Nantes
DOB(R)MAN (Fabien Landry), 28, Nantes
KOA (Olivier Cramm), 29, Lille
DEUCE (David Pageot), 26, Nantes
SENSEI (Damien Boutruche), 30, Nantes
Mr ZLIP (Olivier Loyen), 30, Nantes
KARL (Mathieu Barrabe), 28, Paris
www.level-art.com

4

all with backgrounds in the graphic arts, and does highly advanced and relevant work, underpinned by its cross-disciplinary personality, embracing graffiti (with artist Deuce), graphic design and illustrations on all kinds of support.

Modus operandi

Although the collective is tight-knit, each member tries to develop his/her individual hallmark, and each set of techniques and artistic path is respected. This probably gives the group its strength, because their creative ventures are never mapped out – they always flow from a collective energy, albeit one in which the lead protagonist's graphic identity is palpable. Llor, the girl in the group, Strom, who created the outfit, graffer Deuce and lat-est arrival Koa, as well as Sensei, Dob(r)man, Mr Zlip and Karl, switch between commissions and self-initiated output. Operating solo, in pairs or a group, they exploit their diverse skillsets in the widest possible range of events: exhibitions, illustrations, stickers, prints, magazine pages, merchandise, fabrics... Like many new-generation artists, Level Art transcends the frontiers of art, bestriding disciplines and relishing their participation in myriad projects.

Limited editions

Despite the underground flavour of their output, disseminated via non-institutional networks (they don't show in museums, for instance), Level Art is open to exhibitions: *We try to do one or two big ones a year. Next in the diary are Hamburg in early 2006, and Nantes, Paris, London and Milan with "Pimp my Doll", which we're staging with other French and international artists*. Here again, the diversity of the collective's portfolio is reflected in their project themes: the *Make Feet Beautiful* exhibition (custom espadrilles!) led by graphic designer Sokkho, toy design (arty items and screenprinted cuddlies), and also the design of skateboards, basketball shoes (Vans and Springcourt) and clothing (Spootnick, Angel Dust, the Pébroc collection)... it's all profile-raising, creativity-fostering grist to the mill. In the same vein, the collective readily markets spin-off products to keep the association going: T-shirts, frisbees, dolls, stickers, posters, cushions, badges, you name it – and always in limited editions!

1

1. blason DS project,
vectorial image by DOB(R)MAN &
STROM.
2. series of logos by
STROM/DOB(R)MAN/DEUCE.

2

3. canvas (acrylic/spray/collage),
self-originated, by MR ZLIP.

4. original 175 g ultimate FRISBEE
by SENSEI (limited edition).

5. STROM prédec sticker.

8

constantly foraging

Level Art's creative and visual realm is a combination between several disciplines – graphics, illustration, photography – and societal trends such as skating, comics and extreme sports. There are no guidelines, just mutual trust: *Each member's got their own style and identity, but you can't really talk in terms of specialties because we've all had more or less the same artistic training. We get together occasionally to review what we're doing – and the rest of the time we communicate via our internal forum, because the collective's members are based in Nantes, Paris, Lille and Toulouse.* Level Art is thus a many-headed monster, constantly foraging for trends and feeding on whatever it finds, wherever that may be.

making images

Such a modern way of working – in a network, with different supports and fields – takes a system able to cope with and harness all the energy that's generated. At Level Art, they work a lot with computers and graphics tablets.

Though everyone has their own recipes, they define an initial canvas: *Obviously we work a lot on computer, combining photos, scans, drawings and paintings. We do a lot of pencil sketches to start with, and we're fairly strict about typographic rules.*

The result is always rich, graphically powerful, and appreciated by their peers: in *War of Monstars*, a book featuring 75 illustrators from around the world, their output has a freshness and fire that promises much. *In three years most of us have produced lots and made lots of progress. And it's just the beginning!* You readily believe them.

1. custom skateboard by LLOR.
2. "kubota", T-shirt design by LLOR.
3. custom sk8 HI VANS by MR ZLIP.
4. NDJ skateboard by STROM.
5. NDJ skateboard by STROM.
6. custom skateboard by MR ZLIP.
7. level ART badge series.
8. custom sk8 HI (self-originated project).

1

 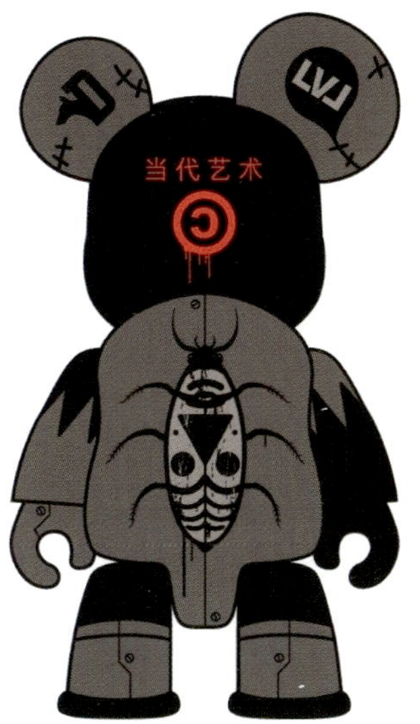  

2

3

1. puppet by STROM (for a themed show).
2. qees template design (project by DOBERMAN).
3. custom puppets and toys by KOA.

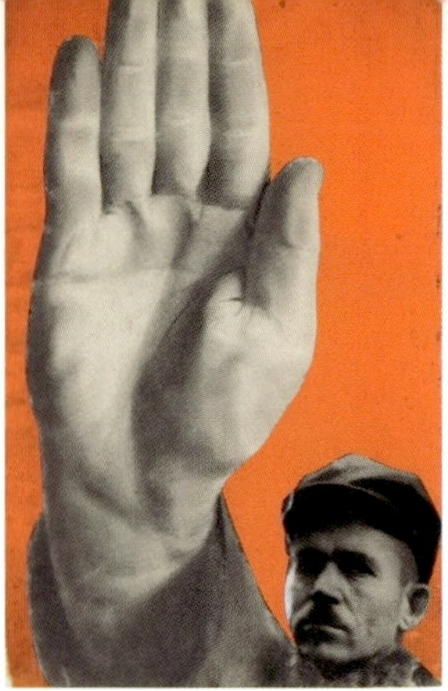

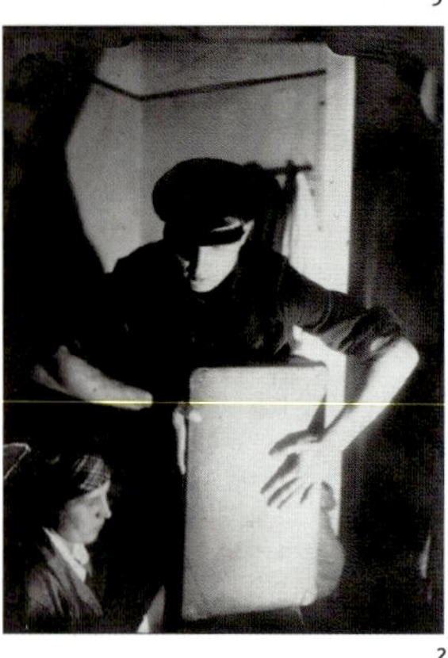

1.2. "socialist reconstruction", a poster based on a (specially taken) photo of klucis and his wife valentina kulagina, also known for her work as a typographer. 1927.
3.4. First rough and final draft of the poster "working men and women, all help to reelect the soviets!" The same visual was used in the poster "under Lenin's banner, for socialist construction" (see p.126). 1930.

klucis
—and photomontage

A **Latvian** artist who settled in Moscow, Gustav Klucis bound the fate of his life and work to that of Russian communism in the 1920s and 1930s. Though a supporter of **constructivism**, he remained an exponent of the technique of photomontage by Étienne Hervy

Though it has its singularities, Klucis' output is primarily a response to the evolution of the artistic and political ideologies that marked the early years of the 20th century. The main shift during this time? Art focused on graphic design, with the creation of posters and books. Artists engaged their art in their era. Changing lifestyles and values, industrialisation and urbanisation generated a need for an avant-garde culture, as previous models fell by the wayside. Throughout Europe came a stream of movements and concepts (the phenomenon of the "isms") up until the apogee of Constructivism – whose first signs, in the shape of Futurism, developed in Russia and Italy, where in 1909 Marinetti called for a *typographic revolution*. Art acquired an intellectual dimension and grew closer to literature. The poster, henceforth, would be a declamatory picture. Provocation was preferred to aesthetisation or neutrality. In its inspiration and dissemination, posters would aim to plug into the here and now and the street, rather than eyeing posterity and museum collections. The easel fell from favour, and was sometimes even rejected: the crucible of artwork was now the printworks. Working with Malevitch, Klucis came close to Suprematism. In this movement, abstraction split from representation, and the creator

РАБОЧИЙ И
РАБОТНИЦА
ВСЕ НА ПЕРЕВЫБОРЫ
СОВЕТОВ

5

6

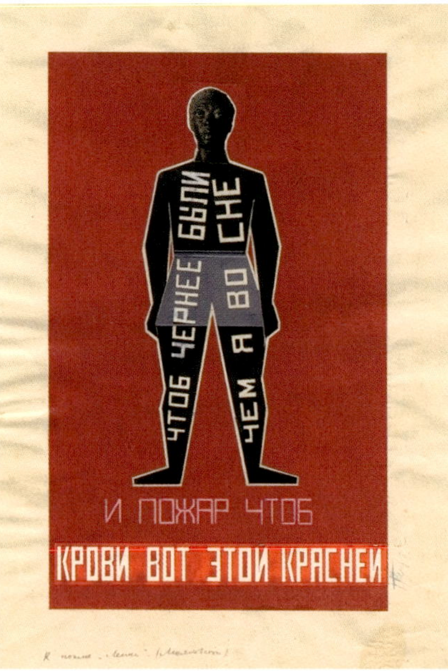

7

5. Photomontage, Lenin's appeal: "Working men and women! Join the ranks of the Russian Communist Party – the party of Vladimir Ilitch!". 1924.
6.7.8. Illustrations for a poem titled *Lenin*. Its author, Mayakovsky, frequently assisted in the creation of constructivist images. His suicide, in 1930, is often considered to have marked the end of the movement. 1925.
7. "May they be blacker than me in dreams, and may the fire be redder than this blood."

of *White Square on White Ground* advocated an economy of means, simple geometric forms and a small range of colours: mainly black, white and red. Klucis retained this palette and the diagonal lines that structured his Constructivist work and photomontages. In 1919, Malevitch quit as director of the Second Free Art Studio and pronounced the end of Suprematism. In the same year, he showed his *White on White* series; in the same exhibition, 18-year-old Alexander Rodchenko showed paintings of black on black. Abstraction, suspected of intellectual leanings, was deemed too distant from the reality of the proletariat – neither portraying it nor giving it a role. Constructivism's time had come.

revolution in motion

Political history has had a marked influence on art movements. World War I caused the poster's development as a propaganda tool, hybridising archetypes of humankind and allegory. The advent of Bolshevism radically reshaped the artistic perspective. After many purely intellectual or incomplete revolutions, the October Revolution was real enough. An entire nation and country adopted a new order. The Constructivists' work would be the images of a revolution in acts. Responding to commissions from those in power, Klucis, a convinced communist, created[1] posters but also illustrations and items of architecture: stadium stands, and panels for exhibition pavilions. He contribute to critical thinking through essays and shows (LEF, October Group) and by teaching colour and graphics.

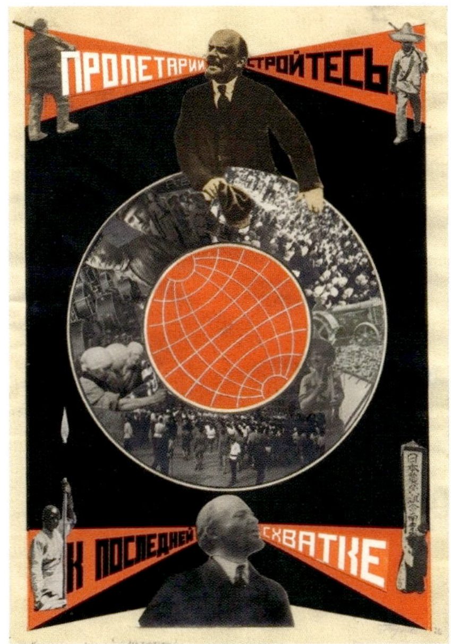

8

9

10

8. "Proletarians, join ranks for the last battle."
9. Screen/platform devised by Klucis for the 4th Komintern congress. 1922.
10. Similar styling for the platform on which Lenin stands in this illustration, "The Young Guard". 1924. In both designs, the same revolutionary concern: to convey and amplify the socialist message.

Photomontage: propaganda art, educational tool

The Tatlin tower project for the 3rd Internationale, or the stands and "radio announcers" that Klucis presented in 1922,[2] attested that Constructivism was meant to be taken literally: it was all about building the objects and propaganda to disseminate the ideas and order of communism, and would flow from it. Building, actually and figuratively. The same gesture marked factory plans and cheered on its operation in posters. Imagery and type was architectured, geometric and driven by contrasts. The proletariat was on the march, and the accompanying images conjured that movement and action with oblique lines and circles. Splitting from abstraction and paint, photomontage was the tool that enabled Constructivism[3] to execute its designs and adopt a utilitarian mood. Photos were treated as the image of the industrial age – a rough-edged document, objective rather than aesthetically-led. It fixed the subject rather than sketching it. Following on from collage (which used a variety of materials), photomontage refocused exclusively on photography. Its expressiveness was achieved by assembly, which Klucis compared to the cinema and its multiple planes. *Photomontage arranged formal elements – such as photos, colour, slogan, lines and planes – to attain a single goal: a more plastic effect.* This quest for effectiveness was an active ingredient that helped institute the new communist order: building towns and educating the masses. Whereas Rodtchenko deployed

11

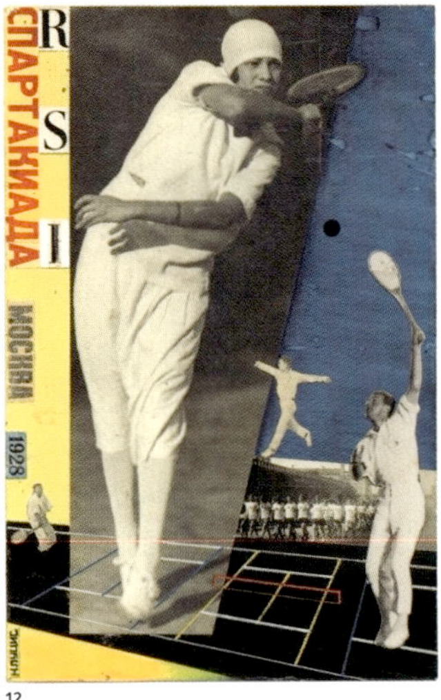

12

13

11.12. Postcard designs for the Moscow spartakiade. 1928.
13. Poster: "young communists, take part in the sewing campaign!", 1930.
14. Cover of *A working woman in the united states*, a book by Rahil Holtman, Gosizdat. 1930.
15. "The death of Lenin", an illustration for the young Guard, 1924.
16. Poster: "under Lenin's banner – For socialist construction!", 1930.

the process for advertising, photomontage for Klucis was *the New Art of propaganda [...], a mass art form in its own right, the art of the edification of communism*[4] and could not be envisioned without a political slogan. Copy functioned in attention-grapping mode, at once slogan and caption. It was inscribed in chunky, sometimes outlined type, often set to contrast with the flat colour blocks that dramatised and guided the image. The proletariat was represented either by crowd shots depicting the popular masses, or by portraits of archetypes: peasants, miners, sportspeople. In some photos, Klucis and his family even performed these roles, alongside more legitimate workers. These emblematic figures, doomed to anonymity, were often joined by that of Lenin, elevated by scaleplay to the status of monumental and paternalistic commander, haranguing and educating the people. Production facilities and industrial machinery naturally feature in the pictures – at once the frames, actors and scenic mechanisms into which Klucis breathes life via geometric assembly and play on perspectives. Pictorial effectiveness was akin to industrial productivity.

Deconstructivism

Come the 1930s, Constructivism went into decline. Like Stalin's politics, the regime's images seemed to refocus on a single perspective. Klucis adapted and straightened his photomontages, stripping out overly structured compositions (the last relics of abstract paintings) in favour of more narrative and

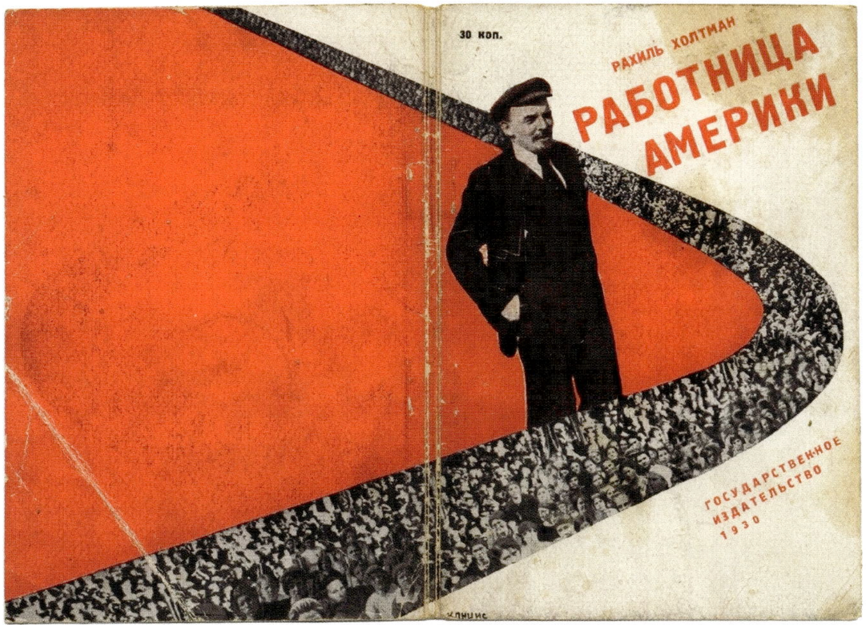

14

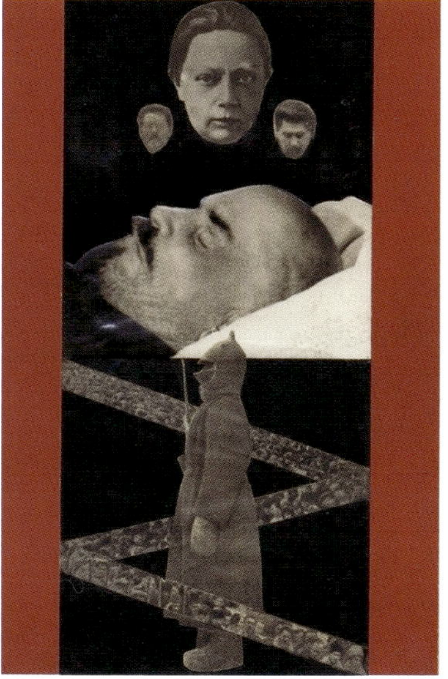

15

16

biography

A Latvian who fought as an infantryman in the Russian army during World War I, Gustav Klucis took part in the Bolshevik revolution and then became one of Lenin's inner circle.[1] In parallel with his political and military commitment, Klucis studied art[2] and in 1918 did his first commissions. The new regime established national free art studios (Svomas) notably led by Kandinsky and Malevitch,[3] which Klucis joined in 1919. His output stretched from the end of his studies in 1921 to his death in 1938. The ex Red Army infantryman and volunteer machine-gunner was shot on 26 February 1938. He had been arrested a month earlier for belonging to an armed group of Latvian terrorists. The truth only emerged in 1989. In 1956 a first rehabilitation included the annoucement to his widow that Klucis had died from heart trouble in a labour camp in 1944.[4] The recent exhibition at the Musée d'Art Moderne et Contemporain in Strasbourg has now put the record straight.

1. The figure of Lenin occupied a prominent place in Klucis' images.
2. First under the Tsarist regime at Riga art school, then at the drawing school of the imperial society for the encouragement of the arts, in Petrograd. A member of Stalin's inner circle, he took part in a workshop for "Latvian red artist-riflemen" at the Kremlin.
3. Pevsner succeeded him in 1919.
4. This date is given in many articles and history books.

Article sources:
• Gustavs Klucis, collection of the national museum of Latvia; exhibition catalogue, containing essays by Emmanuel Guigon, Blanche Grinbaum-Salgas, Margarita Tupitsyn and Irena Bujinska; Éditions des Musées de Strasbourg;
• L'Avant-garde russe, Jean-Claude Marcadé; Flammarion;
• History of the Poster, Josef and Shizuko Müller-Brockmann; Phaidon;
• The Russian Experiment in Art, Camilla Gray; Thames and Hudson.

"The studio was founded to fulfil the artistic requirements of the revolution; it will be a machine-gun in the hands of the working-class…"[5]

ornamented scenes. He continued to do photomontages intended mainly for the monumental panels used as political and cultural event backdrops. Although he produced watercolours in his final years (at the age of 41, in 1936), what really curtailed Klucis' output was a political, not an artistic, factor. After a trip to Paris in 1937, he fell victim to Stalin's Latvian-targeting purges (which claimed 70,000 lives).

1. By himself or with Sergei Sienkin, with whom he founded the "workshop of the revolution".

2. At the 4th Komintern congress.
3. And of its parent Dada, notably practised in Berlin by John Heartfield.
4. Title and excerpt from an essay by Klucis, first published in 1931 and reproduced in the exhibition catalogue. In The Art Front: the class struggle on the spatial arts front, a collection of declarations by the October Group.
5. Klucis on his "Revolution studio". Later, Grapus and then Cornel Windlin would use this metaphor for graphic design as a machine weapon.

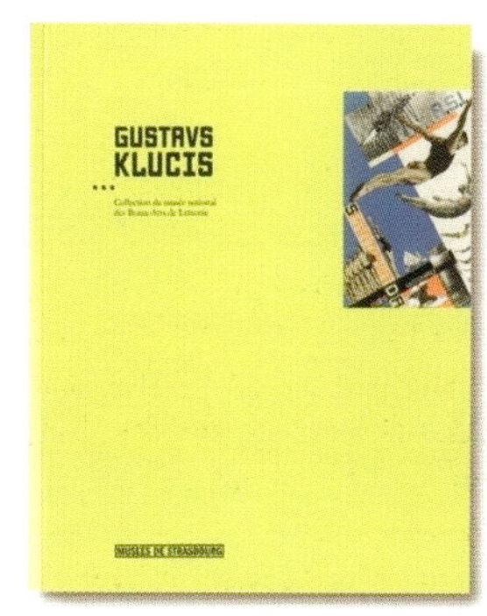

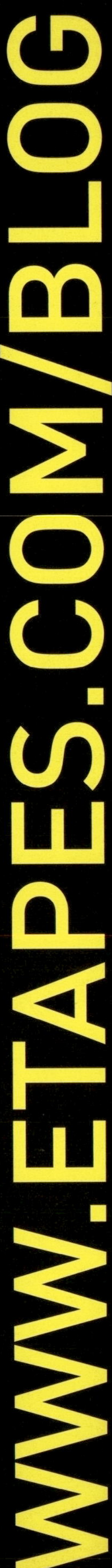

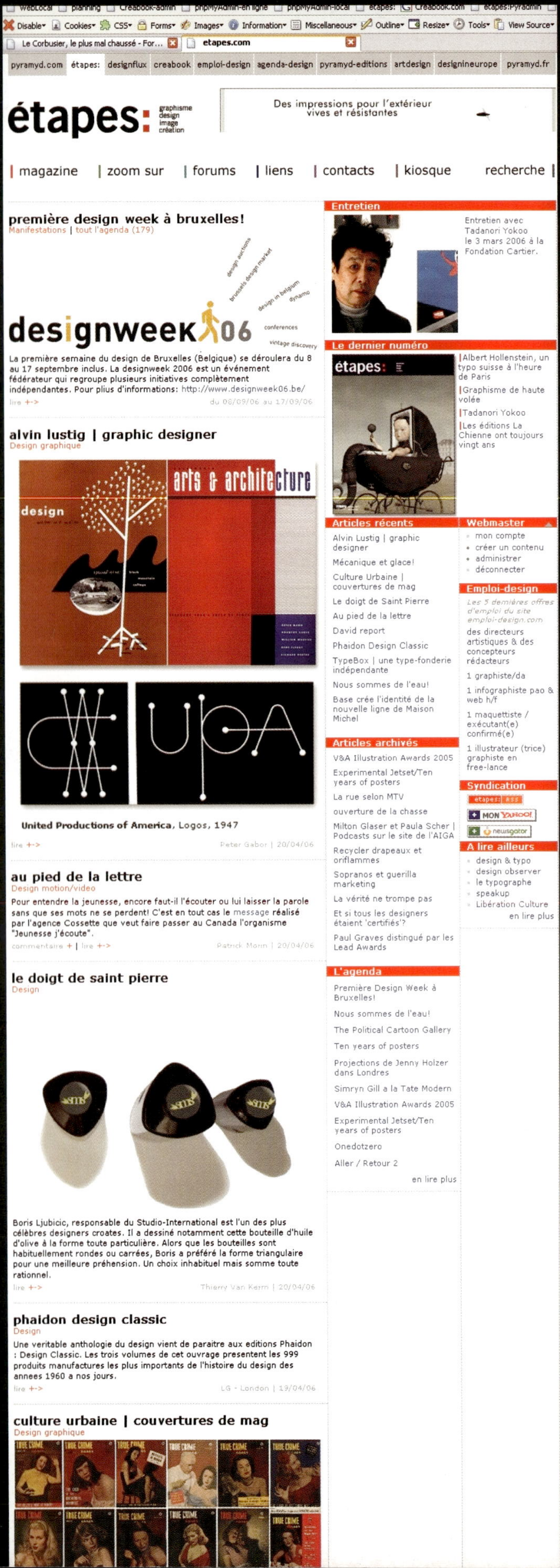

pyramyd.com étapes: designflux creabook emploi-design agenda-design pyramyd-editions artdesign designineurope pyramyd.fr
étapes: graphisme design image création
Des impressions pour l'extérieur vives et résistantes
| magazine | zoom sur | forums | liens | contacts | kiosque recherche |
première design week à bruxelles!
Manifestations | tout l'agenda (179)
designweek06
La première semaine du design de Bruxelles (Belgique) se déroulera du 8 au 17 septembre inclus. La designweek 2006 est un événement fédérateur qui regroupe plusieurs initiatives complètement indépendantes. Pour plus d'informations: http://www.designweek06.be/
lire +-> du 08/09/06 au 17/09/06
alvin lustig | graphic designer
Design graphique
United Productions of America, Logos, 1947
lire +-> Peter Gabor | 20/04/06
au pied de la lettre
Design motion/video
Pour entendre la jeunesse, encore faut-il l'écouter ou lui laisser la parole sans que ses mots ne se perdent! C'est en tout cas le message réalisé par l'agence Cossette que veut faire passer au Canada l'organisme "Jeunesse j'écoute".
commentaire + | lire +-> Patrick Morin | 20/04/06
le doigt de saint pierre
Design
Boris Ljubicic, responsable du Studio-International est l'un des plus célèbres designers croates. Il a dessiné notamment cette bouteille d'huile d'olive à la forme toute particulière. Alors que les bouteilles sont habituellement rondes ou carrées, Boris a préféré la forme triangulaire pour une meilleure préhension. Un choix inhabituel mais somme toute rationnel.
lire +-> Thierry Van Kerm | 20/04/06
phaidon design classic
Design
Une veritable anthologie du design vient de paraitre aux editions Phaidon : Design Classic. Les trois volumes de cet ouvrage presentent les 999 produits manufactures les plus importants de l'histoire du design des annees 1960 a nos jours.
lire +-> LG - London | 19/04/06
culture urbaine | couvertures de mag
Design graphique
Entretien
Entretien avec Tadanori Yokoo le 3 mars 2006 à la Fondation Cartier.
Le dernier numéro
Albert Hollenstein, un typo suisse à l'heure de Paris
Graphisme de haute volée
Tadanori Yokoo
Les éditions La Chienne ont toujours vingt ans
Articles récents
Alvin Lustig | graphic designer
Mécanique et glace!
Culture Urbaine | couvertures de mag
Le doigt de Saint Pierre
Au pied de la lettre
David report
Phaidon Design Classic
TypeBox | une type-fonderie indépendante
Nous sommes de l'eau!
Base crée l'identité de la nouvelle ligne de Maison Michel
Articles archivés
V&A Illustration Awards 2005
Experimental Jetset/Ten years of posters
La rue selon MTV
ouverture de la chasse
Milton Glaser et Paula Scher | Podcasts sur le site de l'AIGA
Recycler drapeaux et oriflammes
Sopranos et guerilla marketing
La vérité ne trompe pas
Et si tous les designers étaient 'certifiés'?
Paul Graves distingué par les Lead Awards
L'agenda
Première Design Week à Bruxelles!
Nous sommes de l'eau!
The Political Cartoon Gallery
Ten years of posters
Projections de Jenny Holzer dans Londres
Simryn Gill a la Tate Modern
V&A Illustration Awards 2005
Experimental Jetset/Ten years of posters
Onedotzero
Aller / Retour 2
en lire plus
Webmaster
mon compte
créer un contenu
administrer
déconnecter
Emploi-design
Les 5 dernières offres d'emploi du site emploi-design.com
des directeurs artistiques & des concepteurs rédacteurs
1 graphiste/da
1 infographiste pao & web h/f
1 maquettiste / exécutant(e) confirmé(e)
1 illustrateur (trice) graphiste en free-lance
Syndication
A lire ailleurs
design & typo
design observer
le typographe
speakup
Libération Culture
en lire plus

In this section, the titles and standfirsts are set in Kievit by Michael Abbink at FontFont (www.fontfont.com) and the body text is in Slimbach by Robert Slimbach at ITC (www.itcfonts.com).

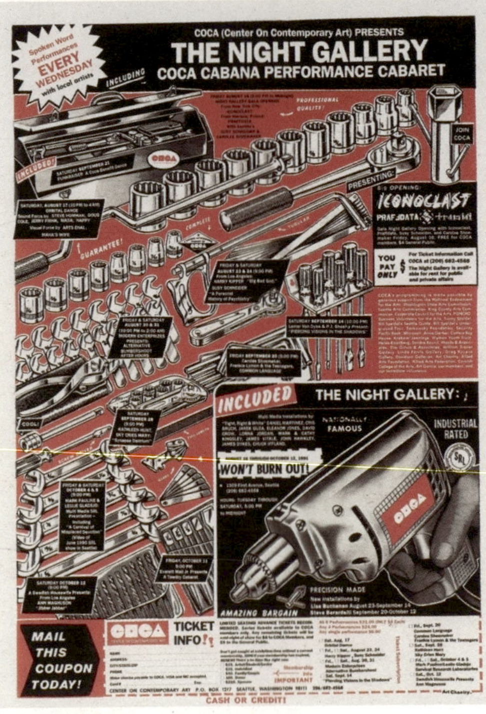

1　　2

— Spirit of Dada, are you there?

The success of the "Dada" exhibition at the Pompidou Centre proved that the spirit of the movement is still alive and kicking. éi proves the point with exhibits of contemporary graphic output from Anglo-Saxon creatives.

1.2. Paris 1922 to Seattle 1991: the use of graphic language common to advertising is, in both eras, an ironic tool intended to shake (one last time?) the corpse of visual creation. Taking a subversive tack, the artists can play with delightful details - such as the photographer, in the composition of Tzara and Iliazd, who turns his back on a pastoral scene to focus on a street urinal; or the electric drill prominent in the announcement of new installations by Lisa Buchanan and Steve Berardelli in Art Chantry's poster.

As recently as 15 years ago, Dada simply didn't feature in books on the history of graphic art. Or rather, its contribution was carefully smothered by those of the artistic avant-gardes that abounded in the early decades of the 20th century – Cubism, Futurism, Expressionism, Suprematism, etc. –, which was a way of denying its specificity and importance: officially restricted to the plastic arts, the Dada aesthetic had to wait until transposed into the framework of visual communication in order to be of genuine interest. The role of history-catalyser was generally deemed to have been played by the Bauhaus – the place where the faintly bonkers experiments of turbulent artists had at last been turned into something useful, and which had managed to meld plastic artists' creativity and manufacturing rigour. This was the thesis put forward in 1989 by Edward M. Gottschall's *Typographic Communications Today*,[1] and which had already been argued six years previously in *A History of Graphic Design*, by Philip B. Meggs.[2] At the time, Dada, along with the Situationist International and punk, were still part of the "secret history of the 20th century" described by Greil Marcus in *Lipstick Traces*:[3] a total aberration in the course of civilisation, which had first needed to be objectified – and substantially sweetened – in order to continue along the path of progress. And with good reason: considering Dada as a constituent of the history of graphic design would necessarily have put a question-mark over the intangible principles of homogeneousness and clarity that were common currency in the visual communication community at the time these books were written – their authors knew perfectly well that, with this chronological presentation, they were contributing to a theoretical and practical definition of the discipline itself. Too shifting, too various, too capricious, too ambiguous… Dada didn't fit the modernist vision then embodied by Massimo Vignelli, Paul Rand, Wim Crouwel, etc., all of them self-proclaimed heirs of the Bauhaus and its synthetic, pared-down, positivist ideal – the plastic arts as reservoirs of novel forms, and the applied arts as processes to rationalise visual innovation and make it profitable.

Back to disorder

Cue a radical change of stance: in 1998, in the catalogue[4] for the exhibition "Graphic Design in the Mechanical Age", co-staged by the Williams College Museum of Art in Williamstown, Massachusetts, and the Cooper-Hewitt National Design Museum of New York, Deborah Rothschild, Ellen Lupton and Darra Goldstein made Dada the main source of graphic design in the 20th century; and described the movement's output as the backbone of an exhibition crafted from the collection of the famous patron Merrill C. Berman. Rothschild, in particular, contributed a chapter titled "Dada Networking: How to Foment a Revolution in Graphic Design": in it she adopted a highly inclusive logic which involved affirming the Dada artists' place in the disciplinary field of graphic design because they used its technical resources (typography, rotogravure, lithography, and half-tone engraving) and distribution channels (posters, press, publishing).

This shift is of tremendous importance, but less for how Dada is perceived than for what it reveals about the serious changes visual communication underwent circa 1990 – and especially in the United States, where theoretical and critical work on graphic-design history is notoriously more intense than in Europe. If Rothschild, Lupton and Goldstein can so smoothly reincorporate Dada into the historical and theoretical framework of graphic design, it is precisely because what had previously made it so odd – and kept it irretrievably off-limits in the corpus of 'serious' design works – became in the space of just a few years the stock-in-trade of contemporary graphic output. The critical perspective on Dada, its creations and heritage radically changed between 1983 and 1998 because graphic design itself radically changed: the dominance of the leading Modernists cited above was called into question and ultimately annihilated by the 'new generation' of David Carson, Rudy VanderLans, Katherine McCoy, April Greiman *et al* whose design practice owes much to values and procedures clearly more affiliated with Dada's legacy than with that of the Bauhaus – especially in the form largely revised, corrected and expurgated of its ambiguities by post-war functional dogma. Nothing changes: writing history is about describing the present.

Contexts and texts

Dada's return to favour in the narrative of graphic design – bursting forth into the family of visual communication, having previously been just some vague, patently weird third cousin – seems therefore to be driven by a strong sense of symmetry between the no-holds-barred experiments being conducted by the mischief-makers in Zurich, Hanover and Berlin and the iconoclastic works of contemporary post-modernist graphic design. The most remarkable aspect of the phenomenon is the conceptual, if not formal, proximity of the graphic objects being produced, although the two movements' contexts have scarcely been likened to one another: there is no possible comparison between the exiles of the Cabaret Voltaire, in refuge in Zurich to flee the butchery of World War I – Alsatian Hans Arp, who had refused conscription into the Kaiser's army, Romanians Tristan Tzara and Marcel Janco, German Hugo Ball and his companion Emmy Hennings – and the radical graphic designers gravitating around the Cranbrook Academy of Art, British and American indie music labels, the Walker Art Center in Minneapolis, and Californian skateboard magazines. And yet…

Let's try exploring a few connecting avenues: on one hand, the rejection of words which characterised Dada – words such as 'nation', 'fatherland', 'honour', etc., over which Europe had ripped itself apart during the four years of the Great War; on the other, work on the arbitrariness of language and the ambiguity of its forms, highlighted by Jeffery Keedy or Katherine McCoy, inspired by the analyses of Roland Barthes and Jacques Derrida. The poems of Hugo Ball, based on onomatopoeia, stuttered syllables and 'negro' language, and the poster constelled with incoherent letterings co-designed in 1923 by Kurt Schwitters and Theo van Doesburg, find their equivalent in the incomplete, transient, apparently undecided typographic forms of Elliott Peter Earls: put simply, the absurd parody of articulated language that is Ball's glossolalia, and the ironic diversity of forms employed in the same page by Schwitters and van Doesburg, can be substituted by the computer copy-and-pasting of bits of disparate letters to reform a single typeface just as eclectic and demonstrative. The clarity and fixity of words' meanings is, therefore, run into the wall by their vehicle itself – accumulation with Ball, Schwitters and van Doesburg, and Frankenstein-esque grafts with Earls.

Images of common consumption

Likewise, it's striking to realise that the enterprise of using electric shock treatment to wake up art (for the Dadaists) and graphic design (for the post-Modernists) involves appropriating the language of the most mundane and predictable commercial advertising: we know, for example, the theory – never really stated explicitly – that "Dada" was originally the name of a hair lotion made by Zurich firm Bergmann & Co., and the anecdote about Kurt Schwitters discovering the term "Merz" when he picked up a bit of a Hanover KommerzBank prospec-

3. The names suggestive of typefaces created by Elliott Peter Earls (Dysphasia, Dyslexia, Dyspepsia, Subluxation, etc.) refer to a sick, gangrenous language which Theo van Doesburg and Kurt Schwitters had already tried to flay in 1923 in their small poster *Kleine Dada soirée*.

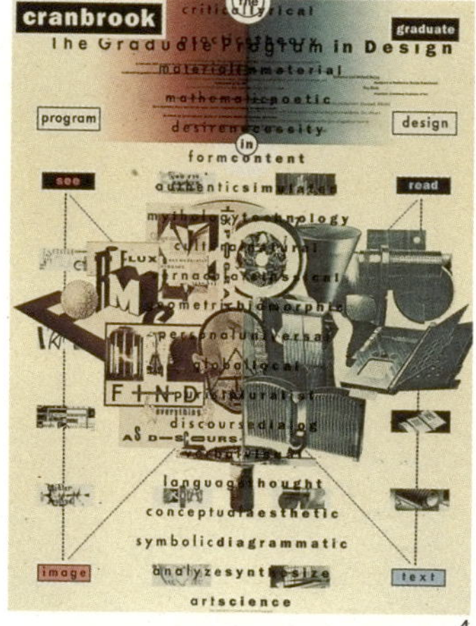

4

5

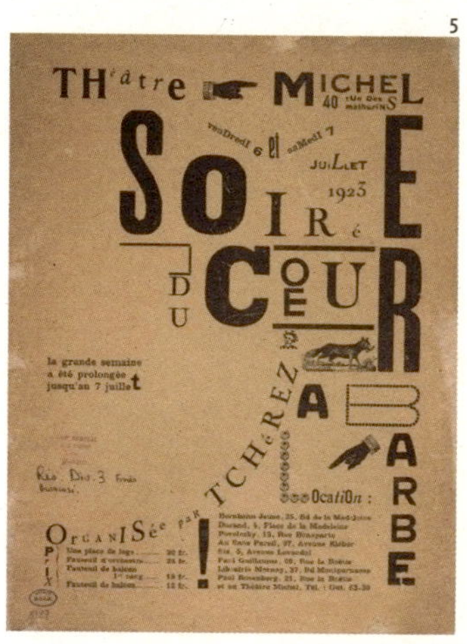

6

7

tus in the street. The 'happy accidents' would be extended in the Paris productions of Tristan Tzara and Ilya Zdanevitch (known as Iliazd), for instance, who at leisure recycled equipment of jobbing printers: decorative typefaces, vignettes engraved on wood, tailpieces, etc. It's an approach that was clearly echoed decades later in some of Art Chantry's work, notably his famous poster for the Center on Contemporary Art in Seattle (1991), which entirely recycled a toolstore ad.

In a related register, the fragmented aesthetic of the photocollages of Raoul Hausmann, John Heartfield and Johannes Baader, which revealed an original critical stance vis-à-vis the photographic image and its media status – as a vehicle of objective, undeniable, descriptive and clinical truth –, has enjoyed an amazing comeback in recent years, with, for example, the album covers created by Julian House, of London studio Intro, for English rock band Primal Scream. The graphic set-up for the *XTRMNTR* album plays with the unsettling and highly expressive character of dismembered and reformed photographs, whose deliberately imperfect assembly is 'supplemented' by flat blocks of colour that function as mysterious gaps – intriguing abstract areas, opaque fragments which, one thinks confusedly,

must be 'hiding something'. This evocation of paranoid feelings, sometimes called to mind by the wartime footage aired by rolling news channels, comes across as a distant reflection of the compositions of Berliner Hannah Höch, such as *Haute Finance* (1923) and *Da Dandy* (1919).

End and means

In photomontage, unlike rigged photographs, the manipulations must remain visible so that the paradoxical tension between the 'photographic truth' of the material and the unrealism – spatially, in particular – of the final results achieves maximum intensity. This special aesthetic coheres with other Dada pieces that place great emphasis on what one might call the 'metronymic effect', i.e. they display a visual aspect in which the production process remain strongly apparent – not to mention the famed operations that conceptually prevailed over the nature of the definitive image. The cover of issue 4-5 of the *Dada* journal, published in May 1919 in Zurich, was a textbook study: it shows a composition of imprints of clock parts, created by Francis Picabia, whose worth lies as much in its evocation of a fixed, denied, abolished era as in its constitution of the visible results of an utterly absurd and pointless activity –

the dissection of an alarm clock, which Picabia conducted in his Zurich hotel room one morning in January 1919, while waiting for Tzara and Arp, en route to meet him for the first time.

This metonymic dimension can still be found regularly today in certain works of the ever-restless Stefan Sagmeister, who has himself provided a clue on this subject in the poster he designed for his own show in Chaumont in 2004 – he featured a quotation by British musician Brian Eno, which starts: *A good way to make something original is to use a method so tiresome that nobody has ever tried it before.* And that is precisely the appeal of his best-known accomplishments: the back of the poster for the AIGA's "Jambalaya" conference (1997), whose text was handwritten or glued-on bit by little bit from printouts; the famous lettering/scarring of the poster for his lecture at Cranbrook (1999) – in this precise case, there is a twofold metonymic dimension, for on top of the evocation of a particularly time-consuming 'graphic' method is that of the self-inflicted cruelty of such a process; and more recently, the poster for the 2003 Adobe Design Achievement Awards, whose apparently pixellated picture is actually made up of 2,500 plastic cups of coffee with varying proportions of milk! While the graphic form of the Dada works has aged, their mode of conception – intensely pleasurable in its gratuitous absurdity – seems anything but extinct.

1. Edward M. Gottschall, *Typographic Communications Today*, International Typeface Corporation/MIT Press, Cambridge, Massachusetts, 1989.
2. Philip B. Meggs, *A History of Graphic Design*, John Wiley & Sons, New York, 1983, 1992, 1998.
3. Greil Marcus, Lipstick Traces: *A Secret History of the Twentieth Century*, Harvard University Press, Cambridge (Mass.), 1990; French translation published by Éditions Allia, Paris, 1998.
4. Deborah Rothschild, Ellen Lupton & Darra Goldstein, *Graphic Design in the Mechanical Age*, Yale University Press, New Haven and London, 1998.

8.

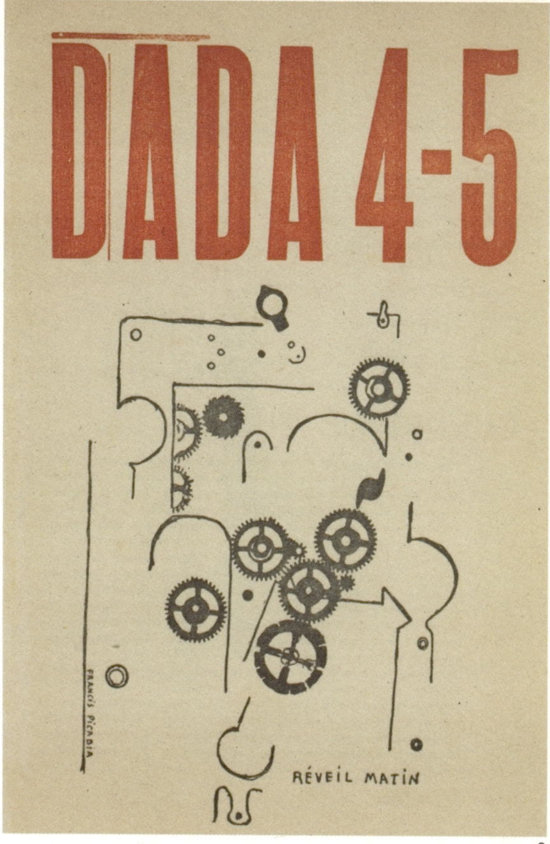

9.

8.9. The method used to construct Sagmeister Inc.'s poster for the Adobe Achievement Awards strongly recalls, in its 'weird work in progress' dimension, that of the cover of issue 4-5 of *Dada*, conceived by Francis Picabia: the maniacal arrangement of the coffee cups on the photo-studio floor has an undeniable kinship with the patient, obstinate and utterly pointless dismembering of the Dada alarm clock.

10.

10. A scene from *Cœur à gaz*, the play penned by Tristan Tzara which provided the centrepiece of the last Dada soirée in Paris: the rigid costumes designed by Sonia Delaunay stopped the actors from taking part in the punch-up that broke out on stage between the Dadaists and the future Surrealists, including André Breton and Paul Éluard.

_ Packaging: France vs Japan

What issues are at stake when packaging is designed? Gérard Caron umpires a match between the highly contrasting outputs of France and Japan, and scrutinises cultural idioms and behavioural rationales.

1. Chocolate: an original opening method

In Tokyo last November, I celebrated my 85th trip to Japan with my local agent Hatsumi Hizawa. I cannot claim, however, to know all of the country's secrets. Let's just say that, over time, I've acquired reflexes and instincts that guide me towards what suits this market. No more, no less... But for a designer it's indeed a privilege to be accepted in this country – truly a spiritual home of packaging, as well as of other riches, of course.

Yet there's a paradox here that some of my industry colleagues have flagged up: *How have you been able to set up Caron Design Network, which works with the best Paris-based design agencies on corporate identities and packaging for Japanese clients, whom you describe as the world's most demanding? Listening to you, one gets the impression they have everything they need in Japan.*

I've encouraged these peers to go to Japan, and they've all come back with the same observation: in Japan, the standard of packaging design is higher than in France!

So, why enlist French creatives?

Lars Wallentin, in my view the person best informed about packaging on our little planet, has just published a piece on admirabledesign.com: in it he declares straight out that French designers currently lead the field in the packaging arena (and food packaging in particular)!

That statement, I think you'll agree, was worth considering in a little more detail. Hence the idea of a joust between France and Japan, along the same lines as car testbeds!

Before conducting this virtual head-to-head, I sought the opinions of Japanese designers and marketing chiefs and did likewise on the French side, to avoid excessive subjectivity and bias – well, in theory...

I selected seven tests:

Test 1: cultural foundations

Offer a carefully packed gift to a French person and a Japanese, and observe. Their behaviours are conspicuously different.

The French person will hurriedly tug on the ribbon and tear off the paper, prettily decorated with golden garlands... whereas the Japanese will take as much time as necessary to untie the ribbon, use his/her nails to peel off the sticky tape keeping the pack closed, and then delicately unfold the paper decorated with golden garlands...

But is it fair to say that one is acting like a savage and the other is highly civilised? It's an important question with regard to packaging. In reality, no, it's not fair. The French person is displaying their haste to discover the contents, and expressing their joy and impatience; the Japanese, through their respectful behaviour, expresses how attentive they are to the gift! The Japanese's behaviour reflects a purely cultural issue. To him/her, the wrapping is the visible part of the gift; it is far more than simple packaging, it is the gift itself, hence the need to handle it with care. In Asian philosophy, there is no structural difference between inside and outside, between body and mind, between food and medicine (it's the same word), etc. the yin is in the yang and vice versa!

In Japanese shops, you find gifts of low retail value with sumptuous wrapping.

Through its culture of gifts and origami – the art of paper-folding, which dates back to the 17th century – Japan pays far more attention than France to

packaging ... and logically wins this first round hands down.
Winner: Japan

Test 2: production and finishing

Here we considered the quality of materials, production generally, and print.

From the outset, things looked bad for the French because of one simple fact: the Japanese spend far more money on packaging, for the reasons mentioned above. In terms of cost-quality ratio, the result would probably be a draw, given that printers and other technical providers in France and Europe have made great strides in the past decade – just look at supermarket shelves today compared to those of 10 years ago!

Having said that, some production techniques are not yet accessible in Europe, particularly certain treatments of plastic and aluminium packaging. How so? Once again, the cost of investing in the machinery, and, consequently, demand which in Europe doesn't exist or isn't met. Too expensive! Keep trying!

Another financial reason lies in Japanese business logic. The country's standard of living – one of the world's highest – means it's possible to market costly, and therefore high-margin, products via a distribution channel still protected from the hard-discounters. Japanese consumers are so hungry for new products that brands refresh their packaging at a rate unheard of in France. Every year, for example, new beers are launched. When was the last time a new beer hit the French market?

With the advent of products made in neighbouring China, and the opening of everything-costs-Y100 shops, i.e. 70 eurocents, the landscape is set to change. But note that even during the crisis caused by the bursting of the financial bubble, Japanese consumers still sought quality and luxury. Yet there is one area where the French rule the roost: perfumery. From the start of the production chain through to design, France has unmatched savoir-faire. Japanese brands, such as Shiseido, are opening plants in France!

To conclude: France, despite the cost-quality ratio that handicaps its designers, and despite the progress made by retailers and the country's supremacy in the area of perfumes and luxury goods, must bow down to the flawlessness of Japanese packaging, whose quality of execution – in every product category – strikes all visiting designers.
Winner: Japan

Test 3: ergonomics and usage

When Lars Wallentin talks about this in his lectures, he starts by unwrapping a Japanese chocolate bar and packet of biscuits. It takes two seconds. Then he does the same with the equivalent French brands: he struggles with film that rips badly, unfindable pull-tags, invisible tearing notches, and so on.
Who hasn't come across an excessively well-sealed top-film on a pack of ham, a box of clingfilm whose teeth don't cut, or bottles of mineral water that only a rugby-player can wrench open, etc.? I believe that 40% of French packaging is not carefully conceived in terms of ergonomics and usage. Compared with its Japanese counterpart, it's simply not up to scratch. You might think this reflects France's generally low investment in packaging. That is only half the answer; the other half is how brand responsibility is defined. In Japan, a purchased product merely initiates the user/brand relationship. If an incident occurs with the packaging or product, the company feels guilty and loses face: it must immediately repair or improve it. In production plants, packaging is constantly refined until perfect. The customer lays down the law.
In our culture, products are there first and foremost to be sold. Never mind companies' grand mission statements – customers can just try their luck with after-sales service… In another area, the hotline syndrome in France is a telling reflection on our mentality. There are exceptions, of course, but not enough to offset Japan's (second) immaculate performance.
Winner: Japan

Test 4: information communication

Here we look at the information given to consumers at the time of purchase and for usage. This may take several forms, and isn't only textual:
– text, of course;
– presentation visuals (e.g. photos, drawings);
– advice for use;
– method of use;
– ingredients;
– nutritional details.
Packaging is now acknowledged as a medium. We have come a long way since the 1970s, when people used to stare at me when I uttered this self-evident fact!
French packaging has achieved huge progress in this area – driven by legislation, certainly, but also by pressure from consumers and brands advocating

2. Manga power.

3. The refinement of traditional packaging.

4. In Japan, everything gets wrapped up: loose goods are a rarity.

5. Detail of cake packaging. You buy two small cakes, presented in a box. At home, you open the box and find: a plastic spoon; a divider between the cakes; a bag of artificial ice; a serviette; and a wrapper with each cake!

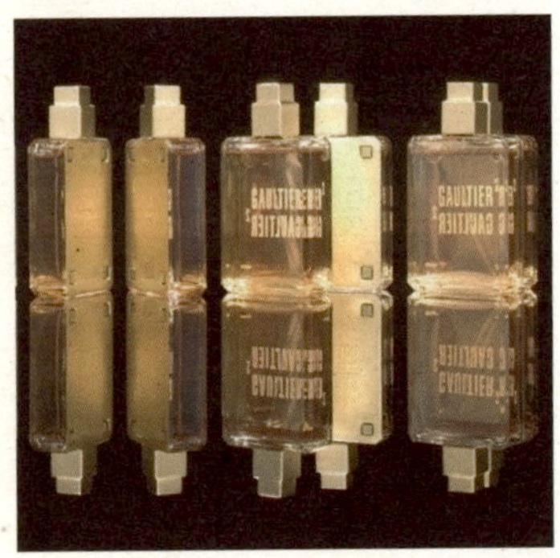

6. Perfumery and French savoir-faire (design: Cent Degrés).

more transparency, traceability and advice. Take one remarkable example: the Fleury Michon range, which gives a whole array of interesting information on composition, the presence of certain beneficial ingredients, conservation times, cooking times, etc. The visuals also strongly demonstrate the content of the pack, but are not exaggerated – even though, in design terms, the brand still has work to do! The food sector in France is particularly innovative with the media dimension of packaging, and there are many examples of this.

What about Japan?

The standard is the same as in France, but the means are different. There, mascots, sketches and mangas are used to explain, with great textual economy. In addition, the facing visual is always explicit when saying what's in the product. A confectionery product with a filling will systematically be shown sliced, with the ingredients listed on one side, and the individual wrappers (if there are any) represented, etc. This will all be photographed with perfect lighting. Evident here is the Japanese obsession about detail! It's a prominent feature of this society: nothing is left to chance. Signage is everywhere; subway-train loudspeakers continually announce the station you've just stopped at, your possible connections, and the next stop. Not to mention the omnipresent advice to be careful, which Westerners soon begin to find unbearable! In packaging, this is translated in the special care paid to the consumer. In creative meetings, you can easily spend two hours on a pull-tag, working out the best place to put it and what colour it should be! Time to look at the scorecard: five years ago, Japan would have won this test by a mile – and today still wins, but only by a short head…

Winner: Japan

Test 5: impact

Faced with a new product, consumers are mainly subject to two types of impact which will capture their attention:
– visual impact, which represents the packaging's 'shout', its power of attraction;
– emotional impact, which engages the senses and influences the irrational dimension. On the reality of the store shelf, these two impacts are obviously closely linked. NB: I'm only distinguishing between them for the purposes of this match, with the arbitrariness that this entails!

To a French person, some Japanese packaging may seem confused and cluttered: text at the top, at the bottom, on the left and right, little visuals here and

there… But the Japanese occupy space differently from us. Not convinced? Look at a Japanese street map! They are read from left to right but vertically too, and, with people now learning Latin characters, from left to right and horizontally; i.e. you can enter a facing – just like a magazine cover – from any side, depending on which signs are used; and as the fashion is to combine Japanese signs with English or French text, you can imagine the result! However, this does not apply to high-end and luxury products, which, as we'll see, play the minimalist zen card!

With regard to the other type of impact, which I'd describe as emotional, the perfection of packaging production, the perfect photography, and the systematic showcasing of the product, often out of context, are not conducive to this spontaneous response; don't forget that we're in a culture where displays of emotion are not part of good manners and savoir-vivre. A neutral expression is de rigueur: no hint of sadness, happiness or fatigue. In a way, this reserve is echoed on Japanese packaging, with the notable exception of the mangas on packaging aimed at children.

French packaging does not have to endure this cultural restraint. Imagery is most often appetising, suggestive and even provocative. When it comes to attracting attention, anything goes.

In terms of visual impact, I can't give either contestant the nod. But in terms of triggering emotion and arousing sensations, *l'équipe tricolore* is ahead!

Winner: France

Test 6: new concepts

The high-powered French retail arena, one of the most competitive in the world, generates incessant demand for innovations, launches and packaging initiatives. The race for new product and packaging concepts is ongoing.

In Lars Wallentin's view, this situation explains French success in creating new concepts, particularly in the area of fresh and ultra-fresh products.

So, advantage France? Not so fast… We've seen that the French are driven to innovate because of the ruthless competition between retailers and the battle between manufacturers and own brands.

In Japan, brands must innovate all the time, but under pressure from consumers! In *combinis*, a kind of convenience store which have a fairly big share of the national retail spend, 3,000 products are changed yearly out of the 5,000 listed!

So it's a close run thing... but the point has to be awarded to France, which has a policy of branding many ultra-fresh products (salads, meat, vegetables, etc.) whereas in Japan the perishable-goods section is full of perfect but anonymous packaging. Quantitatively, France wins it; but qualitatively, this round's a tie.

Winner: France

Test 7: luxury and prestige

Although France is universally acknowledged to be the birthplace of luxury goods, I would suggest Japan is on a similar level. The packaging of traditional cakes, gift teas, fabrics, gift fruits and French pastries is absolutely remarkable in its perfection. It would be criminal to throw it away! But who can name a Japanese luxury brand? Mikimoto pearls, perhaps? But their cases and packaging are pretty dowdy failures... Here we have one of the paradoxes of this refined country, so attentive to production standards. Unlike France, it hasn't known how to export its savoir-faire in luxury and prestige goods, even though domestic demand is considerable.

Japan – soon to be overtaken by China – is the number-one market for the likes of Chanel, Gucci, Louis Vuitton and Dior. There is a real taste for French *grand cru* wines, unknown regional specialities and insider brands (these are true luxury), which are featured in articles and specialist magazines in Tokyo.

Clearly, France is ahead here. Not because its expertise is superior, because, in my view, design and execution are on a par, albeit in different areas. But – and this is where the gap exists – French designers have a long tradition in luxury, which can be applied to many and varied categories: cosmetics, accessories, perfumes, champagne, wine, cognac and other spirits, gastronomy, etc.

Such is the talent available in France that Japanese manufacturers, as we've seen, hire French agencies to design certain high-end cosmetics and perfume packaging.

To illustrate the situation, compare cosmetics designs in the two countries. French designs and packaging are more glamorous and varied, whereas the Japanese offerings, though extremely well made, are creatively less original.

This explains why Japan scooped round two (finishing) but surrenders first place in this round, which rewards creativity.

Winner: France

Conclusions: Japan's the winner

Japan: 4 wins, France: 3 wins
Japan emerges the logical winner in areas such as "cultural foundations", which favour packaging research, and "production and finishing", the consequence of higher investment; but also in the areas of ergonomics and consumer information. These two criteria denote the faultless attention paid to consumers during and post purchase! The French need to make a serious effort in these areas.

France bounces back in the conceptualisation, the intellectual part of packaging – and this is a serious asset in the globalised world. Impact, the fruit of a skilful blend of power and charm, has become one of the attributes that French designers handle deftly. So bravo! Expertise in these areas was long the preserve of Anglo-Saxons.

That France wins the luxury-goods round will surprise no one. But it's still astonishing that Japan doesn't excel in this segment.

This was a close match that reflects the high quality of Japanese packaging in general as well as the huge progress France has made. The score would have been far more lop-sided in Japan's favour in the early 1990s.

Now, just one more push...

7. A creative concept (design: Logic Design).

8. The tradition of French luxury (design: Dragon Rouge).

9. Typographic perfection (design: B & G).

_ Of mice and women

We know what a pin-up is. But we're perhaps less aware it is designated, primarily, by its mode of attachment. To pin up: to fix an image to a wall using drawing or other pins. Pin-ups are aptly named, being subjected to the walls of teenagers' bedrooms or, more scabrously, to the recesses of truckers' cabins. Here was a ready-made form of exposure (as much as it was an iconographic model) for cinema advertising. It brought forth and multiplied ad infinitum girls who, when they tipped back their heads, accentuated their bust still further. Here, [1] 1950s star Silvana Mangano undeniably backs up her proposition.

And now we have a new-style pin-up.[2] The substrate she is featured on – a mouse mat (no tittering at the back)[1] – clearly influences what this character means to us. No provocative breasts, no 'mediological bait' to uncover with relish. On this 28cm x 20cm image, a blonde with half-screen skin, cropped at the beholding eye's start-point, turns round to give me her message: "Roll me over babe!" Bottom right: "Fuji Diskettes" and the firm's logo. The proposition couldn't be clearer: I am invited to discard the two-dimensional (and inert) blonde in favour of the tease she purports to be. Is she not inviting the mouse, and hand, to wander?

Tactile imagination takes over from visual appeal in the Aérelle ad [3], which seeks similarly, and no less stupidly, to pull the wool over our eyes. It's an old chestnut: the optical-mental system, by which desires and reality strangely switch, is akin to trompe-l'œil – which, as we know, can cheat both mind and eye.

Qualification is called for: although the Fuji diskette girl doesn't possess the pregnance which, when we look at certain pictures, tempts the finger to check what the eye doubts, she is part of a long tradition of illusions that men have invented to subjugate themselves. It's as if the image buff, momentarily mislaying his critical faculties, could fantasise that the girl is actually there, rather than her flat representation. A propos, remember those Renaissance portraits, framed head-on or in three-quarter profile, which 'lack only speech'?

Let's mine this seam further. Although Lucrezia Panciatichi de Bronzino [4] is in a withdrawn pose (in Italian, *ritratto* means portrait), her aura is all the more active because the spectator is, it seems, bound not to eye the lady, and is reduced to subordinate rank! (The VIPs of old knew the game, and their devoted artists willingly played it.) A modicum of reflection tells us that proxemics[2] has continually developed new systems.

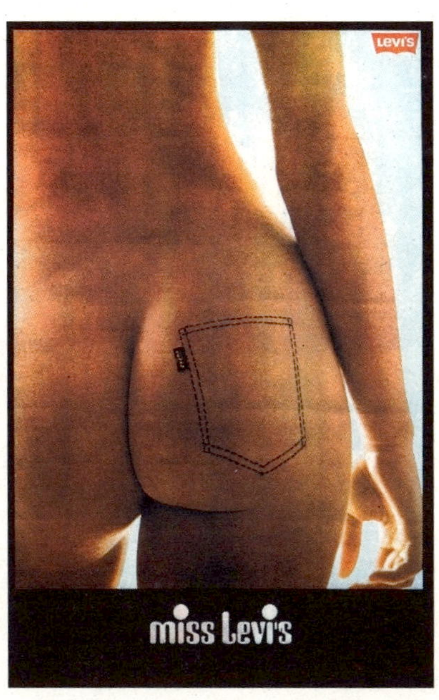

5   6   7

Observe the hook effect – or 'phatic' effect[3] – generated by this propaganda poster from the end of World War I: "I want you for the Navy"[5]. The recruiting officer seems to look 'me' up and down, with an insistent yet reserved eye. The coquette – let's call her Marine – seems to talk to me, whereas in fact she is only addressing my ghost, whom I have delegated to occupy the fictitious place where Marine could pick me up. In short, from mute Lucrezia to comely Marine to the brazen Fuji blonde, the (supposed) solicitation has varied greatly in intensity… only the principle has remained constant – and has been condemned by iconoclasts of every ilk, who beware doubles like the plague.

In passing, it's worth noting that for media work, graphic artists can play it subtle when need be. This point-of-sale poster for Aubade lingerie,[6] is amazing in its finesse and humour. The pin-up, photographed in colour, is just the hung-up (i.e. drying) print of her own person, supposed to have her feet on the ground, which in this case is black and white. In this *mise-en-abîme* composition, the clothes pegs equate to the pin-up pins of yesteryear – but with one, fundamental difference: the pegs are just pictures of pegs. Here, the codes are inverted: for once, advertising rhetoric and critical detachment are pleasingly and intelligently combined.

But back to our mouse mat…

What is the point of this hackneyed (and coarse) artifice of unfulfillable sexual promise? Even an indulgent user can't be fooled. The answer (or part of it at least) is that such a high degree of triviality is now taken tongue in cheek. Agree? Then you will concede that what we have here is the – now conventional – justification for the bad taste which saw Miss Levi's put up in bus shelters 35 years ago.[7] Feminists' blood must have boiled, but the admen doubtless savoured their understatement: these jeans are all you need. Provocation, one realises, is an aesthetic because bad taste has the effectiveness of self-confessed kitsch. By analogy, it is easy to see the Fuji girl as a manifestation of this same kitsch: in the computerised world where women have made a place for themselves, the occasional bout of unreconstructed machismo is undoubtedly enjoyable!

Of the Fuji girl's referents, Roy Lichtenstein's pop art is obviously one of the more prestigious.

Here, *Shipboard girl*, lithograph, 70 x 51 cm, 1965.[8] Two codes which the American painter particularly prized – a kind of close framing and the benday dot screen[4] – have remained specific features of his work, characterising certain comic-strip panels as much as the drawing of our venal blonde.

Code one. Like Lichtenstein, the adman has used

8

9

10

the cliché of the close-up: borrowed from films, it reduces the world to macroscopies. Consider this panel by Stan Drake: [9] the heroine's face, by its very proximity, gives me 'an eyeful'. I am suddenly promoted to the rank of confidant, into the intimacy of the character, who isn't afraid to whisper her secrets to me.

Code two: the screen. The skin of the faces – especially that of comic heroines – is often rendered by the (pink) optical mix of a grid of combined colours: white and red (which aren't always discernable with the naked eye). This pointillism, specific to cheap US comic strips, and magnified and transposed in Lichtenstein's pictorial register,[8] has retained a fascinating quality: in an indissociable whole, it induces a feeling of cold (the mechanical inhumanness of the printing process) and of heat, if not torridness, i.e. the quasi-tactile fantasy of grainy flesh. If our Fuji girl wasn't so small (just 28cm x 20cm…), she would further enhance the sensual effect: the mouse mat (a peripheral object), in obeying the character's order ("Roll me over, babe"), will smooth the screen of the face, as if to homogenise its embodiment. From the standpoint of pragmatics[5] the mouse, invited to be 'enterprising', is far from merely functional. Held by the hand and roving over the mat, it gives me a grip on the screen. And if you accept the analogy between the mat (with its rounded edges) and the electronic computer screen, then also present is the idea that the screen is given material form by the mat perimeter: the screen pixels suddenly equate to ben-day dots… Consequently, can we go as far as to say that the user, as master of the screen, is also the 'master' of the creatures displayed on his strange monitor? We are not a million miles from the myriad girls 'summoned' by draughtsmen (and sometimes talented ones: see Milton Caniff's Miss Lace [10]) since time began, and who are still being undressed under the flimsiest of pretexts.

1. In French, *souris*, mouse, is a slang term for woman - Translator's Note.
2. The study of variations in distance between bodies.
3. Phatic denotes language used for general purposes of social interaction rather than to convey information or ask questions. It is one aspect of pragmatics (see note 5).
4. This process, invented by Benjamin Day c.1870, creates a variety of colour shades and grey shades. It may have been influenced by the work of French theoretician Charles Blanc (*Grammaire des arts du dessin*, 1867).
5. Pragmatics, a discipline derived from linguistics, is the study of relationships between signs and users.

DESIGN**IN**EUROPE 06

DESIGN

GRAPHIC DESIGN

CREATION

COMMUNICATION

TYPOGRAPHY

WEBDESIGN

Published yearly, DESIGN**IN**EUROPE is a business directory and an analytical tool intended for design clients. In the same spirit as *étapes:* magazine, it takes a shrewd and insightful look at the world of European design.

DESIGN**IN**EUROPE 06
aims to be a reference and a design ressource

www.designineurope.com

19,5 x 25 cm - 24,50€ - 208 pages - French / English

To get information on the conditions of publication in **DESIGNINEUROPE 07** (no commitment required), please fill in the coupon below and return it to Pyramyd, 15 rue Turbigo, 75002 Paris, FRANCE.

company: _______________________ job: _______________________

firstname: _______________________ lastname: _______________________

phone number: _______________________ e-mail: _______________________

address: _______________________ zip code: _______________________

town: _______________________ country: _______________________

Cover girls

Illusive - Contemporary Illustration and its Contents

Illusive sets out its stall as an ode to illustration, with the introductory pieces asserting the genre's renaissance as a phenomenon that is now comfortable with photography (or has avenged itself). Illustration has even kicked its dependency on accompanying text. This book is primarily a design anthology (about 150 international illustrators are featured) which stands out by the quality of the selection: plasticity and personal exploration prevail over the ocean of platitudinous commercial illustration. The images (several by each artist) have been grouped in stylistic themes (classic, collage, urban, rock 'n' roll, fashion, childlike...) and are punctuated by interviews with image-makers and agents. It's a fairly accurate survey of the current scene: while the images are sometimes violent and rowdy, they convey the impression of a civilisation insulated in cotton-wool.

The Paperback Art of James Avati

James Avati was a painter more at home on book covers than on canvas. In the 1950s, his artwork fronted a publishing phenomenon: the reprints, by Signet in the United States, of the books of British publisher Penguin. Although Avati calls to mind the realism and documentary spirit of Norman Rockwell's portraits of America, his world seems darker and more sensual. Avati's sleek girls verge on the suggestive, treading a tightrope between innocence and provocation. All they are left with today is the quaint charm of faded jackets of novels by Moravia, Caldwell and Gore Vidal. This posthumous monograph (Avati died in March) is interesting less for the presentation of the paintings themselves than for the insight into their genesis, with the publication of shots taken and used by the painter, who photographed in isolation the various characters and elements of his compositions, and unified them by lighting effects.

The Paperback Art of James Avati
Piet Schreuders and Kenneth Fulton
010 Publishers
28.5cm x 22cm – 200 pages
Colour – English – €29.50

Illusive - Contemporary Illustration and Its Contents
Die Gestalten Verlag
24cm x 30cm
288 pages
English - €44

La Loi et ses conséquences visuelles

The title of Ruedi Baur's latest book (the law and its visual consequences) lends itself to confusion. It is not a technical handbook of charters and legal restrictions (such a document has yet to be written), but rather a look at how a social organisation (contemporary society) interacts with the architectural, graphic and human forms and signs that are part of it. The approach reflects the issues that have concerned Ruedi Baur since 2000, and calls to mind Gérard Paris-Clavel's explorations with non-profit association Ne Pas Plier (do not bend). The book has been produced in conjunction with a philosopher, a politician, a graphic designer, and, in a workshop, with students. The reader can take two paths: illustrations of various themes (police uniforms, legal-text layouts, building outlines, rules of politeness); or searching essays on the representation of power, the role of the visible and of the eye... By way of example, there is discussion of the switch from lookee to looker, for justice in a society in the throes of swapping freedom for security. The book as a whole dismisses the illusion of "by default" or neutrality, encouraging the reader to spot and read the signs in the social (physical or media) space, and invites designers to consider how their work impacts on the wider context, beyond the scope of their commission.

Patterns in Design, Art and Architecture

Flowers, polka dots, abstract or camouflage... Patterns are back in fashion, benefiting from images' new coverability and the rising popularity of ornamentation and illustration. After touching on concrete art and the 1970s, Petra Schmidt (editor of design magazine *Form*), art historian Annette Tietenberg and architecture critic Ralf Wolheim survey contemporary creative output which – in art, design and architecture – draws its essence from patterns. After two essays in reference to *Ornament and Crime* by Adolf Loos, the work of 80 creatives is presented in alphabetical order, in a sober design by Surface, which gives pride of place to large images, simply credited. At the end of the book are more details on each artist (Yayoi-Kusama, Hella Jongerius, and Francis Soler, the architect of the French Ministry of Culture) and their work. Aesthetic pleasure and a simple classification do not prevent a more precise vision of the issues underlying the pattern, according to whether it is used on a surface, in construction or as an ornament (this is Wolheim's area, whereas Tietenberg contributes historical background). In addition, the crossover of disciplines – and therefore of materials and scales – is fully exploited.

Patterns in Design, Art and Architecture
Petra Schmidt, Annette Tietenberg and Ralf Wolheim
Birkhäuser
24.5cm x 34.5cm – Hardback
338 pages – Colour
English – €78.95

La Loi et ses conséquences visuelles
Collective
Lars Muller
Hardback
Colour
French, German – €45

BQuiet...